Knowledge Management
and
Rural Development

Also available

- **Computerization and Digitization of Land Records: Methods and Applications**
  by V. Madhava Rao, R.R. Hermon, P. Kesava Rao and K.L.N. Murthy

---

About the Editors

Dr. M. Padmaja Sudhir presently working as Senior Librarian at the Centre for Media and Rural Documentation (CMRD) in the National Institute of Rural Development (NIRD) is a professional Life Member in the Academy of Library Science and Documentation (ALSD). Her experience is gained from management, computer science, engineering college and University Libraries. Her expertise lies in library management, collection development and knowledge development. Virtual browsing, culling out valuable information and dissemination of the same to the required uses is the focused service.

Dr. Vasala Madhava Rao presently working in the Centre on Geoinformatics Applications in Rural Development at the National Institute of Rural Development, Hyderabad. He did B.E. (Electrical) and an MBA, M.Tech (Remote Sensing) and Ph.D (Spatial Information Technology). He is also a National Committee Member on Watershed, Mahatma Gandhi National Rural Employment Guarantee Act (MGNREGA) programmes for formulation of guidelines and for use of Geo-informatic Technology in Planning, Implementation and Monitoring of MoRD Programmes. He has presented a number of papers in International Conferences and Seminars and has Membership in various International Bodies.

Dr. Rajender R. Hermon presently working as an Associate Professor, in Centre on Geoinformatics Applications in Rural Development, National Institute of Rural Development, Hyderabad. He did his M.A. (Applied Economics and Econometrics) and Ph.D. (Economics). He has guided a large number of M.Sc., M.Tec. and Ph.D. scholars in subject concerning Geoinformatic Applications in Rural Development and Agriculture plan. He has authored several books and contributed papers in National and International Journals.

Knowledge Management and Rural Development

Editors

M. Padmaja Sudhir
Vasala Madhava Rao
Rajender R. Hermon

CONCEPT PUBLISHING COMPANY PVT. LTD.,
NEW DELHI-110059

ISBN-13: 978-81-8069-959-7

First Published 2013

Published and Printed by

Concept
Since 1974

Concept Publishing Company Pvt. Ltd.
Regd. Office:
A/15-16, Commercial Block, Mohan Garden,
New Delhi-110059 (INDIA)
Phones : 25351460, 25351794, *Fax* : 091-11-25357109
Email : publishing@conceptpub.com,
Website: www.conceptpub.com

Editorial Office:
H-13, Bali Nagar, New Delhi-110 015, India.

Acknowledgements

It is a matter of great pleasure to place the present work in the hands of the readers. Paper contributors played a key role in preparing the base for this publication. In many aspects, paper presentation in the workshop is different from publication in a book. This distinction is well identified and suitable efforts are put by the authors in bringing out the publication of this anthology. Our ardent desire of this volume has become fruitful only with the collective assistance received from each individual author. Harekrishna Mishra's thematic paper highlights in bringing out the advantages of best practices of ICT-based knowledge management in agriculture. The article also shows right ways of facilitating to bridge the gap between the world of technology and the world of village environment. We owe a particular debt to him. However, very specifically, we would like to thank those who have given their valuable suggestions towards editing of the volume. Our sincere thanks to all the contributors for their efforts and support to this volume. We are also indebted to the Concept Publishing Co. Pvt. Ltd., who accepted for the publication of this book.

Editors

Preface

Traditionally, communication and exchange of knowledge was possible from person to person or to a group of people. But in modern times with the advent of information technology not only communication of information but also free accessiblility, exchange of information validity to gain qualitatively required knowledge is made possible in rural areas also. Sharing knowledge has more benefits compared to sharing materials. As it confirms one's authenticity in knowledge and increases confidence levels of the possessor. It improves skill development due to the practice one undergoes in sharing process.

Rural areas are structurally disadvantaged in accessing knowledge. To empower them, they must be provided with necessary knowledge through the methods of extension, qualification, research, information and communication. As these facilitate to access, share and utilize knowledge and improve in skill development. Generally, after sharing any material or any aspect of human possession it might perhaps lessen the existing quantity but in contrary the more one shares knowledge the more one strengthens one's and others. This is the underlying idea in all the papers. This is what happens in Raitha Samparka Kendras (RSK) where visitors are farmers to download the information regarding the inputs, cultural practices, marketing avenues, commodity prices, technical suggestions and know-how of the innovative farming practices. A rural tele-centre becomes a knowledge centre when it transfers information into knowledge. To support rural development initiatives, information and Communication Technology (ICT) enabled services and processes have progressed phenomenally.

Editors

The Contributors

Dr. Samwel Kakuko Lopoyetum is a Senior Post Doctoral Research Fellow (UGC-MHRD) in the Department of Cooperation, Faculty of Rural Social Science, Gandhigram Rural University, Tamil Nadu State, India. He has been actively engaged in Post Doctoral research work after the award of Ph.D. degree in Cooperative Management by Bharthidasan University, Trichy. His major areas of interest are Dairy Cooperative Management, Cooperative Banking, Cooperative Education, Extension and Training Development, Project Management, Marketing and Financial Management aspects of Cooperative Sector. To his credit, he has published more than hundred Research Articles on Social, Economic, Management, Education, Cooperative Development and Administration, Cooperative Banking, Dairy Cooperatives, Cooperative Extension and Training Development in the leading National and International Journals. He worked as a Technical Officer in the Ministry of Cooperative Development (Kenya) and Research Associate at the Institute of Development Studies, University of Nairobi (Kenya).

He has published four books and twenty eight research monographs on cooperative management and administration. He has also presented large number of Research Papers and presided over as a Resource Person at the State and National and International Level Conferences, Convention, Colloquium, Workshops, Seminars in India and abroad. He received several awards for the best paper presenter at National and International Level Seminars. He has been actively engaging himself as management and development consultant in various Non-Governmental Organizations, guiding and preparing projects for funding, undertaking report writing for several organizations and preparation of post-tsunami research reports.

Tilak Raj Kapoor Graduated in Civil Engineering in 1976 from MITS, Gwalior. Did advanced diploma in Integrated River Basin Planning and Management.

Presently working as Director, Hydrometeorology, Water Resources Department, Madhya Pradesh. Specialized in Integrated Water Resources Management, Integrated River Basin Planning and Management, World Bank and ADB Procurement Procedures, Information and Communication Technology, Project Management, Financial Management, Knowledge Management, Construction Quality Management, MASSCOT, Irrigation Project benchmarking, Human Resources Development, Web Development.

Dr. Neelam Prasad is Incharge, Institute of Archives at the Indian Institute of Technology, Kanpur. By profession she is a librarian and has been in the library of the institute for many years. She has set up and managed new services in the library, e.g., Computer Aided Reference Service (CARS), retrospective conversion of the library's card catalogue, online journals, etc. Her research findings have been presented in seminars and conferences in India and abroad. Many post-graduate students have worked for their master's dissertation under her. She has a doctorate degree in library science from Banaras Hindu University, Varanasi, India.

Dr. S.M. Vidya Sekhar presently working as Subject Matter Specialist at Central Research Institute for Dryland Agriculture, Krishi Vigyana Kendra (CRIDA-KVK) Hyderabad. Qualified in Agricultural Entimology from N.G. Ranga Agricultural University, Hyderabad. Pursued Ph.D. in Entimology from I.A.R.I., New Delhi.

He put up 17 years of experience (from 1989 to 2005) as Senior Technical Officer, ICAR Headquarters, New Delhi.

Expertise in Crop Management Practices, Plant Protection, Extension Strategies, Training, Documentation, Database Management and Electronic Publishing.

Ms. Shobha Kulkarni is serving the Central Library, IIT Bombay for the last 35 years in various capacities. She is currently working as Head of the Circulation and Technical Processing Section. In addition, Ms. Kulkarni is also working on standardization and correction of bibliographic records in the Library database according to AACR II. She was instrumental in implementing AACR-II rules for cataloguing practice and initiated retrospective conversion project for book database. Her major contributions to the IIT Library include standardization and correction of bibliographic records in the Library database and compilation of journals holdings. Ms. Kulkarni has also worked as a Librarian in *Chitralekha* – a Marathi weekly magazine for the year 1996-97 on lien where she was responsible for creating, handling and retrieving technical and image data.

She has graduated in Science, Postgraduation in Master of Arts and acquired M.Lib.Sc. from SNDT Women's University. Her contributions to the profession are through her association with IGNOU Study Centre, Mulund as an Honorary Programme In-charge for Library Science courses since 1996. In addition, she is also counsellor for B.Lib.Sc., M.Lib.Sc. and PGDLAN courses from 1989, 1995 and 2008 respectively. She is a Resource person for M.Lib.Sc. course in Mumbai University since 1988.

Ms. Kulkarni is Life Member of IASLIC, ILA and BOSLA. She has participated in various national workshops/seminars and attended various short-term courses to enhance her professional knowledge. She has published several articles in conference proceedings and periodicals. Ms. Kulkarni is recipient of Dr. C.D. Sharma award of ILA for best paper presented in 44th All India Library Conference, Hyderabad, 1999 and also Best Paper written and presented award at 5th Annual MANLIBNET conference, XLRI, Jamshedpur, 2003.

Harekrishna Misra is a Faculty in the area of IT & Information Systems at the Institute of Rural Management, Anand. An Electronics and Communication Engineer, he holds a Doctorate from Utkal University, Bhubaneswar, in the area of Information Systems Management. He has about 30 years of experience in industry and academia in the fields of IT infrastructure management, communication and networks. His current research interests include software engineering (process modelling), e-Governance, information systems management in development organizations, e-Business for rural enterprises and ICT enabled value chain in rural enterprises. He has widely published in national and international reputed and refereed Journals. He has also participated in technical as well as programme committees, and has presented papers in national and international refereed academic conferences.

V. Madhava Rao, Professor & Head, Centre on Geoinformatics Application in Rural Development (CGARD), National Institute of Rural Development (NIRD), Ministry of Rural Development, Government of India, Rajendranagar, Hyderabad 500030.

R.R. Hermon, Associate Professor, Centre on Geoinformatics Application in Rural Development (CGARD), National Institute of Rural Development (NIRD), Ministry of Rural Development, Government of India, Rajendranagar, Hyderabad 500030.

Dr. P. Kesava, Associate Professor, Centre on Geoinformatics Application in Rural Development (CGARD), National Institute of Rural Development (NIRD), Ministry of Rural Development, Government of India, Rajendranagar, Hyderabad 500030.

Contents

Introduction

Validity of information is contextual. Information at any context unattended to remain passive. The passive information can get activated when geared up with linked current information. For instance, the past history of a person dead or alive, region, an item or incidence is highlighted when a similar incident occurs in current times.

However, the world of knowledge presupposes information but not *vice versa*. In recent times the growth of information world is redoubled in all respects. There might perhaps be many barriers for not transforming the entire information world into knowledge world. Accessibility, awareness, lack of identification and need are a few to mention acting as barriers. For free flow of information into the knowledge stream, these barriers are to be identified and measures may be worked out to overcome. The National Workshop of Knowledge Management in Rural Development Spectrum is an attempt in this endeavour. The workshop not only defined Knowledge Management in rural development *per se* but has seen the all-round perspective of managing knowledge and confirmed the amended statement of Francis Bacon's expression "Knowledge is Power" into "Sharing Knowledge is Powerful".

The first article details basic issues of knowledge management along with concepts, types, attributes, factors and their components. Managing knowledge incidentally occurs at two levels. Individual knowledge is based on the past experiences and future requisitions whereas organizational knowledge is managed with collective efforts. In both aspects of knowledge management past knowledge is lost through attrition and changes in the individual and organization. Much knowledge and knowledgeable resources remain unidentified, unrecorded, unmodified and unutilized in the absence of the system. Knowledge manager is to develop mechanisms to identify, map internal expertise, record, store and utilize the internal as well as external resources and share these through Intranets for creating value information, according to some educationists is considered as mere acquisition of facts and knowledge as a mental process that takes shape in the mind which has very little or nothing to do with outside elements. Information should not be an end in itself, but should also serve as a means to the end attainment of "Knowledge".

Globally, the utilization of IT is at its peak, telecom and government create demand for holistic solutions. The government involves in urban planning, developing cities, power, and land records, agriculture and forests increase technology application. The content perhaps would be contributed as value added information. Similarly, the online imagery providers like Google Earth create awareness among people about the uses of satellite imagery and GIS data.

A rural tele-centre becomes a knowledge centre when it transfers information into knowledge. For instance, a tele-centre providing market price is an information centre. A tele-centre which enables the rural community to understand differential mechanisms through which prices are influenced and determined is a knowledge centre. Some of the best practices are also discussed. Indian farmers are suffering from lack of right information at the right time. They require timely information on weather conditions, sowing time, availability of inputs, expert advice on maintaining the crop, information on market value, etc. NIC has taken up initiatives in bringing situation demand ICT-led development which includes Web-enabled applications, GIS-based applications, Multimedia applications, Database applications and e-Governance and training, etc.

Best practices of ICT-based knowledge management in agriculture are perhaps the right ways of facilitating to bridge the gap between the world of technology and the world of village environment. This is evident in frontier technologies like biotechnology, ICT, renewable energy technologies; space applications and nano-technology provide opportunities for launching and "Evergreen Revolution" capable of improving productivity on a sustainable basis. Santhosh Kumar insists on better understanding potential and limitations as it is important to recognize the differences between data, information and knowledge. Information and knowledge could be seen as closely related and complementary stages along the same road and as such, both perform essential roles in decision making process. The successful implementation of knowledge management calls for certain strategies for effective rural development. Sufficient ICT-skilled manpower was not available and also facilities for maintenance of the systems were not in place during that time. There should be single point entry which provides access to websites of different departments of rural development, all government information relating to rural development should make available from that site. The site should be used by general public, business men, and employees of private and other government departments. The article "Perspective and Strategies of Knowledge Management in Dairy Cooperative Development" by Samwel describes that dairy sector as a regular and steady income provider and stands next to agriculture and so is the best vocation to achieve higher growth of rural economy. The liberalized economic environment has motivated Indian dairy cooperative industry to deal with competitive dairy trade and commerce (business). The flow of technological benefits and investment in dairy cooperative sector demands for the advance application of knowledge management in the dairy sector. Hence, the applications of knowledge management in dairy cooperative sector assume greater significance in crucial areas such as production of milk, procurement of milk, transportation (distribution), processing, marketing, management accounting system and financial management, etc. Information and communication technology is a vital component (organ) of knowledge based cooperative dairying productivity and sustainability in India.

The most important benefit of the Knowledge Management System (KMS) in the overall enhancement of the dairy farms competitiveness while keeping costs at the minimum is extremely paramount; it improves the organizational responses, timely delivery of dairy products, goods and services into the open market/customer and act as an input to the promotion of research and development in developing countries such as in India and Kenya in the twenty-first century.

It would improve profitability, productivity, production, procurement, transportation, processing, distribution, marketing and sales promotion in dairy cooperative marketing business organizations in the changing dairy business environment. It needs improved use and development of ICT and KM in dairy cooperative industry and would enable them in taking crucial commercial dairy decision making process in the changing dairy business environment. Dairy farming system and milk production system is a subsidiary occupation and it can provide employment opportunities and livelihood to many farmers located in the rural and urban areas.

In the era of Economic Liberalization, Privatization, Globalization and changing business environment it is highly essential to generate "generic" production and marketing strategies for the effective and efficient enhancement of the competitiveness of dairy cooperatives and dairy farmers. It is feared that, import of dairy products will dislodge the domestic market. The globalization process has created an environment leading to the fluctuation in price, marketing system, production system, etc., which adversely affect dairy products, milk production, and dairy cooperative sector.

The flow of technological benefits and investment in dairy cooperative sector demands for the advance application of knowledge management in the dairy sector. Hence, the applications of knowledge management in the dairy sector assume greater significance in crucial areas such as production of milk, procurement of milk, transportation (distribution), processing, marketing, management accounting system and financial management, etc. The software industry is providing new tools to increase animal productivity and create new opportunities for understanding even complexities of dairy cooperative industry, agro industrial system, intensive agriculture, etc. The changing environment is moving towards the era of knowledge intensive dairy cooperative development and agricultural development. This can be effectively done through Rural Knowledge Centres (RKC) across the country.

Vidya Sekhar in his write-up Knowledge Management in Research and Development of Indian Agriculture elaborated that agriculture has become more global in its reach, more complex in trade and exchanges, more technologically grounded and even more challenged with balancing sustainability, productivity, profitability and hence is in inclusiveness. In order to address these issues, a paradigm shift is called for in human resource development, research, technology generation, technology dissemination and commercialization. In this endeavour the conventional research approaches need to be supplemented by the cutting edge technologies requiring multi-disciplinary and multi-institutional inputs. At this juncture "knowledge management" plays a pivotal role. A guiding and inspiring vision of what India has the opportunity to become by 2020 must take into account the enormous productive potential of knowledge to accelerate the development and transformation of the country. India's rate of economic growth can be substantially increased if the country becomes a superpower in knowledge and if the potentials of information and information technology are fully understood and exploited. Efforts must be made to strengthen the informatics in agriculture by developing new databases, linking databases with international databases and adding value to information to facilitate knowledge management and decision making at various levels. Expressing the same Santosh Kumar with the similar opinion said that knowledge management can address from two different perspectives. The first one is more people-oriented as it focuses on people and organizations. The second one places the emphasis on information technologies as enabling technologies. The difference between these two perspectives is the level where knowledge management is applicable. People-oriented knowledge management seeks answers to questions such as "How can we improve the knowledge creation and organization"?, "How can we adapt our communication culture to become more knowledge-friendly"?, "How can we manage our human capital more efficiently"?, and "What methods and incentives exist to foster knowledge sharing and transfer"? The objective of technology-oriented knowledge management is to support knowledge workers in companies at an operation level. That is, information technologies are used as enabling technology to provide the knowledge somebody needs to perform a specific task as efficiently as possible. Often, this requires a careful and smooth integration of knowledge management tools with business process management tools.

Shobha Kulkarni considers knowledge as an essential commodity and feels more so to rural mass as it has become the most vital issue to all Government and Non-Government Organizations working for Rural Development Programmes. In this context the article aims to initiate the role of libraries in Rural Development Programmes by applying Knowledge Management initiatives to develop the Knowledge Management System for rural community development. The knowledge represented in library environment is the full utilization of information and data coupled with the potential of people's skills, competencies, ideas, intuitions, commitments and motivation as the explicit knowledge. Whereas the tacit knowledge is the knowledge created constantly by people, becomes a powerful commodity and the articulation of personal knowledge with technical principles will form the cultural knowledge. She has also elaborated the characteristics and tools for knowledge management. The steps taken in libraries for KM process involve Knowledge identification; Knowledge collection; Knowledge organization; Knowledge preservation and Knowledge Dissemination. It is like a backbone to library manager who may be recognized as knowledge manager to set KM as a strategic priority to obtain users' satisfaction. KM techniques thus entails extracting relevant knowledge from multiple sources along with their context and being able to collate them meaningfully for developing the fruitful relationship between human beings and the captured knowledge. As KM is successful in narrow domain and RD being one of the highly referred domain by Government organizations, it is then the right area for application of KM. Libraries can use KM initiatives as a potential backbone in RD programmes. Jayaprakash, while talking about the working methodology of Village Knowledge Centres also described the Village Resource Centres in detail. The content generation and capacity building are the primary works to develop the community database. The area contains different communities like fishermen, farmers, tribals, etc. So the database has to address various problems from different communities. Apart from that we have a strong database of Ayurvedic field cultivation and practice. We have an expert body to analyze and process data in ayurveda coming from other VKCs and to reply their queries.

The challenges presented are mentioned that apart from the cardiac patients, other streams are also coming forward for treatment which they could not handle at present. The fund for running all this has to be found to some extent from its activities. So we have to plan some fund generating activities for VRC. After a proper field survey about the diseases of this area, we are supposed to request the service of more medical expertise through tele-medicine. Despite dealing with problems putting sincere efforts, the project could not sustain 2009 onwards. The practical aspects of knowledge management in rural development are dealt by Tilak Raj Kapoor in his paper distinctly mentioned the pyramid shaped data, information and knowledge need restructuring as the data directly cannot lead to information and similarly information also cannot lead to the knowledge. There is a need to move away from the traditional model of Data-Information-Knowledge-Wisdom and provide a framework to create knowledge assets without moving through the formal structure. This can best be done through participatory interaction approach. One who observes the environment closely and interacts with it can definitely provide some knowledge assets. In this approach interaction with rural masses becomes key pillar of the knowledge management. The paper is an outcome of vast knowledgebase available on Internet and has been adopted to put the things in a simpler way that can be used by knowledge society for its own Knowledge Management. Neelam has a framework for knowledge management practice in rural development in Indian context. By providing a creative and relaxed atmosphere people can synergize their insight and also update themselves with new and interesting things. Innovations germinate from creative or combination of explicit and implicit knowledge, in addition to developments of ICT. Rural areas are structurally disadvantaged in accessing knowledge. To empower them, they must be provided with knowledge efficiently, through the methods of extension, qualification, research and information and communication technologies. She has analyzed some community projects such as Akashganga (the milky way), Wired villages of Warna, Gyandoot, TARAhaat and E-Chaupals. Similar ICT based projects have been initiated in Pakistan for rural development. Multipurpose community telecentres have been adopted for the purpose of development in education, farming, policy formulation, funding, management, etc. Suresh Babu felt that a culture of knowledge sharing needs to be introduced first and building knowledge maps can be strengthened later. For this purpose, integrated knowledge sharing programmes need to be stimulated. The broader application of ICT has paved way to the new social situations and has emphasized in shaping the public mindset and attitude towards the latest technology. Investment in ICT offers the potential for developing countries to increase exports, create good jobs and diversify their economies. The Department of Information Technology, which monitors and spearheaded the entire system of ICT, operated as the nodal agency supporting every government department in their activities helping them to implement project successfully. The projects such as Mukhya Vahini; Sachivalaya Vahini; SAARIGE; Krishi Marata Vahini; Raitha Mitra are directly implemented by the IT department. Raitha Mitra Yojane was a demand driven agricultural extension system implemented during 2000-01 in the entire Karnataka State. The scheme is aided by both State and Centrally sponsored funds. Raitha Samparka Kendras were established at *hobli* (sub-block) level to meet the requirements of the farming communities. Farmer can visit the Raitha Samparka Kendras during the working hours to get any information regarding the inputs, cultural practices, marketing avenues, commodity prices at different APMC yards, technical suggestion and know-how of the innovative farming practices. In order to make the scheme self-sustain, user charges are collected from the farmers and various public and private sector companies involved in agricultural activities. A farmer who has utilized the services of RSK opined that instead of spending time at the petty shop discussing about the present day political scenario, if we happened to sit at RSK for few minutes, we could get vital information regarding farming.

In the process of information communication the two ends of the transaction, the giver and the receiver exist with the core item information around which the entire process is circled. How best the information is communicated that much perfect would be received by the beneficiary. To hike the beneficiaries, the ICT tools should be user friendly and easy accessibility, affordability and ought to be made to divert the attention of the rural people approach without fear and doubt.

1
Basic Issues in Knowledge Management

Padmaja Sudhir

Knowing ignorance is strength
Ignoring knowledge is sickness
—Lao Tsu

Introduction

Sir Francis Bacon coined the expression, "knowledge is power". For Knowledge Management (KM), the focus is "sharing knowledge is power" (Jay, 2001).[1] Knowledge management presupposes knowledge in people's mind. Basic issue in knowledge management is to identify or locate knowledge in order to capture it. Once the knowledge is captured it can be shared with others. Then, individuals apply this shared knowledge and internalise it using their own perspectives. This might perhaps produce new knowledge, which then needs to be captured, and the cycle starts over again.

Knowledge (K) Capture >>>K Sharing >>>K Application>>>K Creation

Fig. 1.1: Knowledge Management Life Cycle

Knowledge Management is not a discipline. It is another way of improving quality and growth of individual as well as organization. Issues in Knowledge Management (KM) cover how to pursue KM, comprehend it and eventually realize its value. Some consider that any manipulation of knowledge as knowledge management. This strengthens the view that knowledge sharing, knowledge production and knowledge transfer are also factors in knowledge management.

National Knowledge Commission though established on 13th June, 2005 was formally launched by the Prime Minister of India on 2nd August, 2005 with the mandate to advise the Prime Minister on matters relating to institutions of knowledge production, knowledge use and knowledge dissemination to achieve in the twenty-first century which is being termed as "Knowledge Century".

What is Knowledge?

Knowledge is a term, used widely and indiscriminately. Widely because everybody is concerned with it; and indiscriminately as there is no one definite universal meaning for knowledge. It ranges from simple information to absolute mastery over any field of study or original contribution to the theory of knowledge. If one speaks of oneself as "I am not a knowledgeable person in this field", means one who has not reached a level of being "Very High in Regard" so as to be considered oneself as an authority in that field (such as art, education, religion, morality, etc.) Hence, knowledge is a term used with varied meanings depending on different contexts.

A Few Definitions

Knowledge is—

- Justified true belief for philosophers and empiricists who believe knowledge claims can be justified by facts. Any less justified beliefs were called "probable opinion". (Nonaka and Takeuchi, 1995)[2]
- Information in context.
- Understanding based on experience—an idea central to modern pragmatism and epistemology.
- Experience that can be communicated or shared.
- Made up of data and information and hence can be thought of as much greater understanding of a situation, relation, causal phenomena and the theories and rules.
- Composed of and grounded solely in potential acts and in those signs that refer to them.

Knowledge is objective in the sense that it is not agent specific and is shared among all others as an object whether or not they believe in it. It is also not personal because all others have access to it. It emerges from the interactions of all others.

Types of Knowledge

Knowledge is both personal and organizational. It is personal and subjective because it is the outcome of knowing/learning something. Learning and knowing are processes but knowledge itself is the outcome of these processes is not a process. Organizational knowledge is the knowledge of the employees in the organization which is different from the individual knowledge.

Attributes of Knowledge

Another approach to categories of knowledge is whether the knowledge is tacit or explicit Tacit knowledge is knowledge embedded in the human mind through experience. In contrast, explicit knowledge is knowledge codified and digitized in books, documents, reports, white papers, spreadsheets, memos, training courses, and the like. (*ibid.*)[3] "Explicit knowledge can be retrieved and transmitted more easily than tacit knowledge. Because it is knowledge learned directly from experience, tacit knowledge is difficult to share across space and time. The person with tacit knowledge has no conscious experience of what it is that is causing his/her activity. Tacit and explicit knowledge have been expressed in terms of knowing-how and knowing-that, respectively." (Elias, 2004)[4].

Data, Information and Knowledge

Data, Information and knowledge emerge from social process. These may be the overall properties of the institution or the individual depending on the level of focus of analysis. They are inter-subjective constructs. Data are unorganized and unprocessed facts. Data are a set of discrete facts about events—structured records of transactions. (Elias, 2004)[5]. Too much data offers no action plan and no guidance. The individual or the organization need to decide on the nature and amount of data needed to create information. Hence, it is stated that information is extracted and formatted contextually from the relevant data.

The word information is derived from the word *inform*, which means that to give shape to the data. Information is shaping the data to arrive at a meaning in the eyes of the perceiver. Information is an aggregation of data that makes decision making easier (*Ibid.*)[6].

Knowledge is derived from information similar to the way information is derived from data. Knowledge has various meanings depending on the discipline it is used. Basically, knowledge is human understanding of a special interest that may be acquired through study and experience. In other way of defining Knowledge is the processed information. This brings us to the Case of the Misconceived Pyramid. In treating the distinctions among data, information, and knowledge, it is often assumed that these are arranged in a pyramid form with data, the most plentiful type, at the bottom; information produced from data above it, knowledge produced from information through the hard work of "refining" or "mining", above it, and wisdom produced from knowledge, the rarest of all, at the top. This is presented in Fig. 1.1. But if data and knowledge are also information, what happens to the pyramid? Figure 1.2 presents a new picture in it, information is not made from data. Data and knowledge are made from pre-existing information, that is, "just information", data, knowledge, and problems are used in the knowledge life cycle to produce more information including new knowledge. In effect this figure is saying "Get rid of the pyramid, get on to the cycle". (Joseph, 2001)[7].

The roles of knowledge are—

- To transform data into information,
- To derive new information from existing ones, and
- To acquire new knowledge pieces.

Wisdom appearing on top of the pyramid is considered as meta-knowledge. Knowledge management focuses on definition of the context and validation of the information. It also increases the connections among people (who have knowledge) that would likely not occur without the help of a knowledge management.

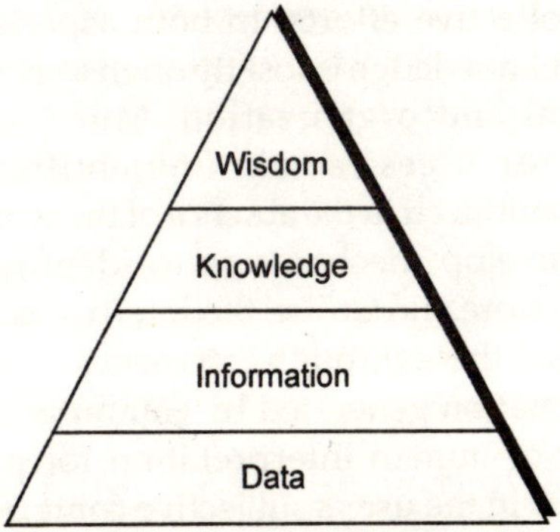

Fig. 1.2: The Data, Information Knowledge and Wisdom Pyramid

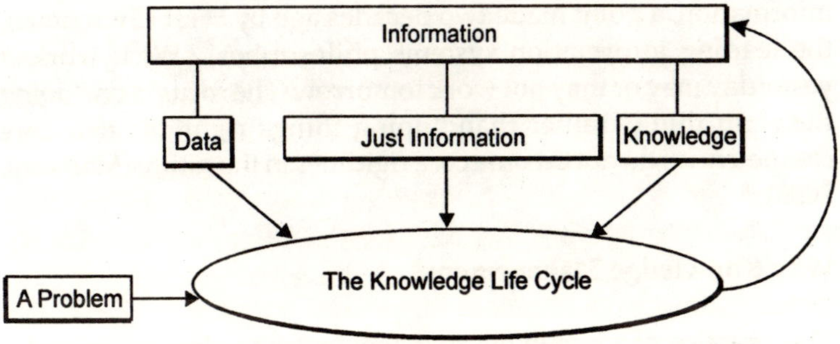

Fig. 1.3: Problems, Data, Information, Knowledge and the KLC

Source: Joseph, 2001[8].

What is Knowledge Management?

Knowledge Management (KM) is a newly emerging, inter-disciplinary business model that has knowledge within the framework of an organization as its focus. It is rooted in many disciplines, including business, economics, psychology and information management. KM means accumulating knowledge assets and using them effectively to gain a competitive advantage (Brooking 1996)[9]. Knowledge management is not a project that begins and ends but is an ongoing attempt and changing contribution in the way an organization operates. Knowledge Management could be viewed in two levels. At individual level one manages one's own knowledge based on the past experiences and future requisitions whereas organizational knowledge is managed with collective efforts. In both aspects of knowledge management past knowledge is lost through attrition and changes in the individual and organization. Much knowledge and knowledgeable resources remain unidentified, unrecorded, unmodified and unutilized in the absence of the system. Knowledge manager is to develop mechanisms to identify, map internal expertise, record, store and utilize the internal as well as external resources and share these through Intranets for creating value.

"While information generated by computer systems is not a very rich carrier of human interpretation for potential action, knowledge resides in the user's subjective context of action based on that information. Hence, it may not be incorrect to suggest that knowledge resides in the user and not in the collection of information, a point made two decades ago by West Churchman, the leading information systems philosopher". What worked yesterday may or may not work tomorrow. The focus is on "doing the right thing" rather than "doing things right" so that core competencies do not become core rigidities in the future (Malhotra, 2000).[10]

Why Knowledge Management?

The practice of knowledge management has already proved a number of benefits and has offered justification for further implementation. Timely sharing of knowledge is facilitated by Internet. By sharing knowledge, an organization creates exponential benefits from the knowledge as people learn from it (Elias, 2004).[11] The purpose of sharing knowledge is to capture the tacit knowledge required for a process and take support to knowledge workers to communicate and share knowledge with subject experts. This kind of sharing knowledge gives inputs to determine which processes are more effective or less effective than others. The fruits of knowledge sharing are intangible compared to knowledge hoarding. Because people starting any project from scratch work need basic knowledge guidance which perhaps resides in any corner of the globe.

Information *vs.* Knowledge

Knowledge management is not based on information. Information becomes knowledge after its use by people in ways that create value. Knowledge is information in action or information in practice. Information is context sensitive and knowledge is consensus oriented (Elias, 2004).[12]

Layman's terminology of knowledge is confined to information. Information, according to some educationists is considered as mere acquisition of facts and knowledge as a mental process that takes shape in the mind which has very little or nothing to do with outside elements. Information should not be an end in itself, but should also serve as a means to the end attainment of "Knowledge".

Information can be referred and disseminated whereas knowledge can neither be disseminated nor referred. Similarly information explosion does not necessarily lead to knowledge explosion.

If the information transmitted to a person can undergo the experience of knowledge then it must also be possible that knowledge can be transmitted as information. One cannot by merely reading the principles of Buddha become a knowledgeable or enlightened person. What one needs to do is to practice them to perfection. Hence, all knowledge cannot be transmitted through information as knowledge because the essence of experience is involved in it.

Emphatically speaking the society is slowly drifting from knowledge-based society to information-based society and human beings have become transponders of information rather than repositories of knowledge. This is because of the revolutionary development of Information Communication and Technology (ICT). Social and economic progress is achieved by many countries principally through the advancement and application of knowledge with the help of Information Communication and Technology.

Knowledge *vs.* Technology

Knowledge Management is not about technology; it is about mapping processes and exploiting the knowledge database. It is applying technology to people's minds. With the explosion of information in the twenty-first century and the new introduction and usage of electronic gadgets impetus of storing, capturing and manipulating images have gained the momentum. It is a fact to state that a computer vision is different from that of the human. Over the past few decades major projects have been undertaken to make computer understand, index, classify and annotate a picture which may represent many ideas, thoughts, etc. Presently, the emphasis is on Context Based Image Retrieval (CBIR) for analysis, matching patterns, clustering objects and for identification. Image information is very crucial in geographical service for public, surveillance, space research, criminal investigation and many others. In this context, the image retrieval has gained impetus with the application of new tools in ICT.

Globally, the utilization of IT is at its peak, telecom and government create demand for holistic solutions. The government involves in urban planning, developing cities, power, and land records, agriculture and forests increase technology application. The content perhaps would be contributed as value added information. Similarly, the online imagery providers like Google Earth create awareness among people about the uses of satellite imagery and GIS data. As there are new usage of current archive and current satellite imagery in disaster management, imagery data can be archieved overtime and may be used for measuring change and the rate of change. 'There are countless areas in which Information and Communication Technologies are being applied to address sustainability issues, even where profit rather than sustainability is the stated goal (Sajid, 2011).[13] Number of programmes have brought GIS and IT closer, and many of the large Indian IT players have started getting into integrated programmes which involves GIS and IT. This is likely to take the geospatial applications to an entirely new space and make them more widespread.

KM in Rural Areas

The rural community has the blend of the new knowledge with the existing traditional knowledge as components of knowledge management. Thus knowledge management necessitates a participatory management in which the rural community plays a crucial role of absorption, validation, critical evaluation, assimilation, understanding and appreciation of information. A paradigm shift in the concept and practices of extension will occur only when the community develops its own framework for knowledge management (Balasubramanian, 2010).[14] A rural tele-centre becomes a knowledge centre when it transfers information into knowledge. For instance, a tele-centre providing market price is an information centre. A tele-centre which enables the rural community to understand differential mechanisms through which prices are influenced and determined is a knowledge centre. In agriculture there is no area in which IT has no role to play. In the light of Globalization and the impact of WTO on agriculture and agro-based industries, the use of IT based services in this field has become imperative. Development in enabling technologies, such as Information and Communication Technology (ICT), Geographical Information System Technology (GIST), facilitate informatics-led Agricultural Development, which will be a step towards enhancing the quality of life of the farming community (Meenakshi and Gayathri, 2010).[15]

KM through Expert System/Artificial Intelligence

By avoiding the geo-spatial barriers it is possible to help farmers to gather together online and facilitate the disposal of their produce at attractive prices. Farmers can be made to go for online bidding for various agricultural commodities. This would perhaps demand to facilitate complicated IT systems, which should be supported by proper infrastructure and post-harvest technologies, storage, etc. Besides, expert systems/AI is at present considered the most successful product of artificial intelligence research. The complex problems confronted by farmers include yield losses, soil erosion, diminishing market prices because of international competition, increasing chemical pesticide costs and pest resistance, and economic barriers hinder the adoption of farming strategies. Hence, farmers need to become expert managers by taking the support of expert systems. User friendly systems, particularly in local languages, can generate interest in farmers. It is also possible to create networks or harness the power of the Internet to make these services available to farmers in all parts of the country. But it is tedious and massive task to generate application packages and databases to cater to the entire domain of Indian agriculture. Efforts could be towards promoting the coordinating agency, which would perhaps play an advisory role and evolve a standard interface for users. This would call for the support of the state-of-the–art technologies, such as remote sensing, geographical information systems, bio-engineering, satellite technology and the like to efficiently manage the agricultural performance. Frontier technologies like biotechnology, ICT, renewable energy technologies, space applications and nano-technology provide opportunities for launching an "Evergreen Revolution" capable of improving productivity on a sustainable basis. In order to ensure social inclusion in access to new technologies, public investment in socially relevant agricultural research should be stepped up under the umbrella of the National Agricultural Research System (NARS) comprising large number of Indian Council of Agricultural Research (ICAR) institutions, state agricultural universities, all–India coordinated research projects and national bureaux (Hilaria, 2010).[16]

Best Practices

Indian farmers are suffering from lack of right information at the required time. They require information on weather conditions in time, sowing time, availability of inputs, expert advice on maintaining the crop, information on market value, etc. NIC has taken up initiatives in bringing situation demand ICT-led development which includes Web-enabled applications, GIS-based applications, Multimedia applications, Database applications and e-Governance and training, etc.

Cyber Dhabas: A large number of access points called cyber dhabas are set up which consists of a PC and modem and an operator. Farmers can take the assistance of the operator for a nominal charge. The problem faced with these is the connectivity, i.e., the dial up lines are very slow to get access points and hence other viable options are required to be explored.

e-Choupal: This is the ICT's web-based initiative and is designed to provide physical service support through a *choupal sanchalak*. He, being a farmer acts as the interface between the system and the farmers.

IFFCO-ISRO Project: The IFFCO-ISRO project experience was the base for extension of more intensive GIS-depended services like creation of databases that contain information of interest to the farmers.

Agricultural Marketing Information Network (AGMARKNET): ICT-based Agricultural Marketing Information Network (AGMARKNET) launched a central sector scheme which links important agricultural produce markets spread all over the country and the State Agriculture Marketing Boards and Directorates. This scheme facilitate wider market access to farm produce and better price discovery through value addition and dissemination of information on market requirements in terms of quality, packing, standards, etc. This was executed with the support of NIC.

Agricultural Extension Information System Network (VISTARNET): To facilitate technology access by small farmer holders efforts are being made to establish "VISTARNET-NICNET".

Agricultural Research Information System Network (ARISNET): The ARISNET links ICAR institutions and their Regional Research Stations, Central Agricultural University, State Agricultural Universities and their colleges, Krishi Vigyan Kendras, Zonal Research Centres etc. ARISNET is now an integral part of agricultural research, extension and education process.

Integrated Fertilizer Management Information System (FERMIS): An integrated Fertilizer Management Information System (IFMIS) of worth Rs. 1.99 crore has been executed through NIC and various IT based systems developed covering, Planning, Movement, Import, Handing-Payment, Project Monitoring, Performance Monitoring and Evaluation aspects to strengthen Fertilizer Informatics for decision support.

NOTES

1. Liebowitz, Jay. Knowledge management: learning from knowledge engineering, United States, *CRC Press*, 2001, 131p.
2. Nonaka, Ikujiro, and Takeuchi, Hiro. The Knowledge Creating Company: How Japanese Companies Create the Dynamics of Innovation, New York: *Oxford University Press*, 1995.
3. *Ibid.*,
4. Awad, Elias M. Knowledge Management, *Pearson Education*, Delhi, 2004, 456p.
5. *Ibid.*,
6. *Ibid.*,
7. Firestone, Joseph M. Key Issues in Knowledge Management, Knowledge Management Consortium International, Inc., Knowledge and Innovation: *Journal of the KMCI*, 1(3), April 2001.

8. *Ibid.*
9. Brooking, A. Intellectual Capital. London: *Thompson Press*, 1996.
10. Malhotra, Yogesh. "Knowledge Management for the New World of Business", *www.brint.com/km.*
11. Awad, Elias M. Knowledge Management, *Pearson Education*, Delhi, 2004, 456p.
12. *Ibid.*,
13. Malik, Sajid. Industry Outlook, *Geospatial Today*, January, 2011, 14-23.
14. Balasubramanian, K. Village Knowledge Centres and Open/ Distance Learning, *Indian Agriculture and Information and Communication Technology (ICT)*, Soundari, Hilaria, M.Ed. New Century Publications, New Delhi, 2010, 197p.]
15. Meenakshi, R. and Gayathri J., ICT and sustainable agriculture development, Soundari, (Soundraria, Indian Agriculture and Information and Communication Technology (ICT) Soundari, Hilaria, M.ed. *New Century Publications*, New Delhi, 2010, 197p.)
16. Hilaria, Soundari, M. Ed. (Indian Agricultural and Information and Communication Technology (ICT), *New Century Publications*, New Delhi, 2010, 197p.)

2

Building Knowledge Management for Effective Rural Development

K.T. Santhosh Kumar

Introduction

"Just as the whole Universe is contained in the Self, so is India contained in the villages"... This has been said by none other than Mahatma Gandhi, the father of our nation and the visionary architect of India's rural development programmes. The villages epitomize the soul of India. With more than 70 per cent of the Indian population living in rural areas, rural India reflects the very essence of Indian culture and tradition. No wonder then that a holistic development of India as a nation rests on a sustained and holistic development of rural India.

India with an area of 3.28 million sq. km is the seventh largest country in the world. In population, which has already crossed the billion marks, it is next only to China. The democratic set-up combined with its billion populations gives the country the unique status of being the largest democracy in the world. India is a union of 29 States and 7 Union Territories. Each State is further divided into districts. There are more than 600 districts in the country. Each district is further divided into smaller administrative units called development Blocks or talukas. A Block may have urban as well as rural areas. While the urban areas consist of towns, the rural areas consist of villages. There are more than 6,00,000 villages in India.

There are three levels of government: the Central Government, the State or Provincial Government and the Local Government. Each of these governments is elected by the people at the national,

State and local level. The Central Government is responsible for administering all the States including Union Territories. Each State or province is administered by a State Government which is headquartered at the State capital. The State governments are empowered to take decisions on subjects listed in the State List. The local government also called local self-governing bodies or Panchayati Raj Institutions. There are two types of local government: urban local bodies and rural local bodies. The urban local bodies are local governments of urban areas and consist of municipalities and municipal corporations. The rural local bodies consist of a three-tier Panchayat system: district Panchayat or Zilla Parishad, Block panchayat and village panchayats.

The Evolution of Rural Development in India

The most important landmark in the history of Indian rural development efforts was the setting up of an organization called community projects administration in March 1952. The main thrust of the organization was to administer community development programmes at grassroot level. The organization and its programmes underwent many transformations. In an effort to accord higher priority to rural development, Department of Rural Development was constituted in October 1974 as a part of Ministry of Food and Agriculture. However, it was realized that for a sustainable development, rural development has to be more holistic and all encompassing, that includes not only agriculture development but also the economic betterment of the people, a better and higher quality of life and social transformation. This realization led to several transformations to the originally conceived Department of Rural Development, in terms of mandate, status and name. Today, the erstwhile Department of Rural Development has been elevated to the status of a Ministry and has been renamed as Ministry of Rural Development.

Rural Development Information System in India

The need for imparting training to the development functionaries has been recognized from the First Five-year Plan and a number of training institutions established at the Central (NIRD) level, State Institutes of Rural Development (SIRDs) at the State level and

Extension Training Centres (ETCs) at regional levels. NIRD has taken up the task of conducting training programmes in order to fulfil the objectives of implementation of multifarious and multidimensional rural development programmes efficiently and effectively and also to reach the benefits of the programmes to the target groups. It is not possible to impart training through class room mode to all the functionaries, especially for grassroots level Panchayati Raj functionaries, and felt that the training should be decentralized at district, Block and village level. In this context NIRD proposed a mode of distance learning under Tenth Plan which is most suited for wider coverage and also to facilitate imparting training in local language with local content. In order to fulfil the objective of widening the reach of coverage of training, NIRD is envisaged to develop a distance learning component in training programmes under the Tenth Plan proposals. The proposed distance learning mode can contain the introductory print material, some components of audio-visual material, video conference or "one-way-video, two-way audio", correspondence by e-mails, field visits by groups and if need be a rap-up session at the local level by personal contact. This mode would have the Internet advantage of enabling the teaching and to communicate with all 25 SIRDs, as well as 88 ETCs, if need be in one single planned interaction programme. Minimum 200 sessions would be needed in a year, if four interactive training sessions are proposed to conduct in a week. It may be seen that the total number of participants spread over 25 SIRDs at the rate of 40 at each node will mean two lakh persons in a year. If in the second phase, the facility is extended to 88 ETCs, the total number of people trained could go up to as high as 8 lakh persons in a year. The operating cost of Rs. 85 lakh per year will work out to a cost of Rs. 11 per participant on an average. Thus, this period for "one-way-video" and "two-way-audio" training facility will be highly cost-effective and will enable reaching out to larger number of participants. NIRD attaches top priority for utilization of the proposed facility as a component for distance education. The representatives of SIRDs and ETCs will be specifically trained in the phased manner in management of the learning centre, responding to the operational parts of the equipment as well as manpower management in order to help free and effective participation. The software design and production will be oriented towards the specific programme being planned for distance learning.

In view of the expertise of NIRD, it is repeatedly possible to develop training curriculum as well as training inputs in various areas including watershed management, ground water development, common property resources, village and cottage industries empowerment of Gram Sabha could be the pivotal programmes cutting across different sectors.

Attempts by NIRD

The National Institute of Rural Development (NIRD) is the country's apex body for undertaking training, research, action research and consultancy functions in the rural development sector. It works as an autonomous organization, supported by the Ministry of Rural Development, Government of India. NIRD established in 1958, emerged over the years as a centre of excellence for research and training in rural development. A key player in the Indian rural development scenario, NIRD also serves as a consultant of international repute in the field of socio-economic development. Research and consultancy studies are undertaken ranging from sustainable economic development, women's development to human resource development, organizational development and non-farm sector besides natural resources management, planning and evaluation. In addition, NIRD's forte is curriculum development, preparation of training manuals and training guidelines. Over 180 training programmes are conducted annually benefiting over 3,000 Indian participants besides 5-6 international programmes attracting 25-30 participants each year from several developing countries from Africa, Asia-Pacific, Eastern Europe, Latin America and Caribbean. Under the 71st Constitutional Amendment the three tiers of Panchayats have to elect nearly 35 lakh representatives once in every five years. These representatives have to be well informed and trained on various aspects of rural development. Additionally the other stakeholders in various policy making bodies, research and training institutions, NGOs and others need also be trained periodically. Naturally, these vast user base, scattered throughout the country, can be covered only by using web technologies.

Knowledge Management

Knowledge Management (KM) is a relatively novel management

concept. It has been pushed by the rapid developments of Information and Communication Technology. ICT facilitates a speedy exchange of data, information and documents. There is groupware for communication; content management systems to organize and retrieve documents; expert systems, data mining and text mining systems, tracing services and search engines, e.g., Google. Communication *via* e-mail, fax, and phone and video-conferences is ordinary business. It is good guessing that technological advances will continue to revolutionize the way we communicate and interact with each other. While the speed and ease to exchange data and information will increase, a new challenge for users emerges: to select relevant data, information and documents.

To better understand potential and limitations it is important to recognize the differences between data, information and knowledge. Information and knowledge could be seen as closely related and complementary stages along the same road and as such, both perform essential roles in decision making process. Wilson (1996) presents a useful illustration that by selecting and analyzing data, information can be produced; selecting and analyzing information can generate knowledge; from this, decisions can be made and action can be taken.

Strategies of Knowledge Management in Rural Development

Successful knowledge management strategies depend on effective partnership and network behaviours at all levels of governance. At a micro level, individual actors need to be equipped with a unique set of skills and capabilities. The successful implementation of knowledge management calls for certain strategies for effective rural development. They are:

(i) e-Governance in Rural Development Sector

ICTs have been in use in the rural development sector as early as 1986. But both the utilization and the impacts have not been so impressive. The agencies were not adequately equipped to exploit the capabilities of the software. Sufficient ICT-skilled manpower was not available and also facilities for maintenance of the systems were not in place during that time. Further, there was not sufficient thrust from the agencies to ensure the success of the project.

Three major developments have been instrumental in heralding the era of e-governance:

- *Growth in Network Technologies:* Advancement in network technologies, in particular the Internet have opened up possibilities for government departments to talk to one-another and also with the citizens and businesses.
- *Software Integration Technologies:* Emerging technologies such as SOAP Protocols and Web Services are making it possible for islands of software solutions to be mainstreamed into an integrated solution. The integration of government business solutions with employee database has helped in bringing about the required amount of accountability.
- *Digital Certificates:* This has helped not only in lending legal validity to electronic transactions but also in securing the transactions that take place over the Internet.
- *Digitization of Local Language Scripts:* This has been an important step in taking the benefits of ICT-usage in government to the people, in particular rural people.

(ii) Developing Models of Providing Urban Amenities in Rural Areas

Knowledge powered rural development is an essential need for transforming India into a knowledge power and high bandwidth rural connectivity is the minimum requirement to take education, health care and economic dynamism to the rural areas. Knowledge society leading to knowledge super power can prosper and survive only in the environment of economic security and internal security. Nation has to work for transformation into 'developed India'.

It is envisaged that rural models to share/augment service capabilities to cater to the IT enabled service demands from local sources. Such models should aim to provide opportunity for rural economic development and prosperity. Youth in the rural localities could be easily trained to cater to requirement of IT enabled service industries. We can get place and manpower at very cheaper rates when compared to urban localities. This will also aid in stopping movement of families towards urban localities. The model envisages a habitat designed to improve the quality of life in rural places and makes special suggestions to remove urban congestion also. Naturally our most demanding urban problem is that of congestion removal and efficient supply of water and effective waste disposal in every locality are the paramount civic needs. There is a minimum size below which a habitat is not viable and not competitive with the existing congested city. At the same time, the existing congested city is not economical compared to a new town once a minimum size of expansion is crossed.

(iii) Strengthening Financial Services in Rural Areas

To deepen knowledge among government institutions on best public policy practices for improving rural financial services. The main objective should be to assist governments of respective state or country to undertake policy reforms needed to increase the supply of financial services in rural areas and to expand access to these services among the rural poor. The deeper understanding among government institutions of the impact of public policies on rural financial services is very necessary. Discussion with main stakeholders in the region on the importance of implementing differentiated policies to strengthen the supply of rural financial services and to increase access to those services among the rural poor should also be taken into consideration.

(iv) Establishing an Internet Portal on Knowledge Management

There should be single point entry which provides access to websites of different departments of rural development, all government informations relating to rural development should make available from that site. The site should be used by general public, business men, employees of private and other government departments. The portal should be designed in such a way that it should be able to give information on all schemes of the government based on category, gender, income, age, qualification and location. The facilities provided to a visitor to the website should include:

- Ability to view details of schemes by selecting the agency and scheme name.

- Facility to search for schemes on the basis of the name of the implementing agencies or district in which the scheme is being implemented; category of citizen to which the scheme is applicable (Scheduled Caste, Scheduled Tribe, disabled, etc.).
- Facility for advanced search on category, age, qualification, location (rural/urban).
- Facility to compare different schemes at a time on the basis of rate of interest, income limit, period of repayment, availability of subsidy and other such parameters.
- Listing of non-loan schemes that do not give soft loans but provide other kinds of support such as technical and marketing support.
- Listing of schemes for groups such as self-help groups; and schemes for self-employed persons implemented by public sector banks, co-operative banks and NABARD.
- List of the documents required for sanction of loan.

(v) Information Plan for Rural Development

The successful implementation of the development strategy demands certain information requirements. The development strategy also clearly specifies where the required information will be generated and who will be target consumers of such information. The information generated varies in terms of type of information, level of its detail, the source at which it is generated and the target where the information will eventually be consumed.

The various types of information such as policy and programme guidelines, fund allocation and disbursement details, details of beneficiaries, implementation or progress details must be included. The source that generates the information, for example, village panchayats, Block panchayats, agencies at village level, NGOs, etc. and more importantly, the target group that consumes the information are necessarily included in the information plan.

(vi) Sustainability of Rural ICT Centres

Rural ICT centres can become sustainable if given time and appropriate support. The time needed will mainly depend on two factors. First, the level of ICT awareness of the general population both in terms of using the ICT based tools and the potential benefits of the ICT tools. The second factor is the presence of reliable and relevant local content. In order to transform rural people's access to computers and Internet into meaningful and sustainable usage, there is a need for raising awareness of :

- the presence of the ICTs in the community
- the use and the benefits of ICTs; and
- the existence of reliable and relevant local content.

The government can play a positive role in the introduction of ICT centres in the rural areas in different ways. These could include, but not be limited to:

- Policies and regulations (e.g., providing incentives for service providers to provide services to rural areas, facilitate dissemination of information between different rural and non-rural ICT centres, etc.),
- Encourage and support the creation of public-private partnerships (i.e., where possible and feasible, purchase bandwidth from the local ISP), and
- Promote the use of ICT tools in all aspects of life (i.e., leading by example, providing different e-Government services, etc.).

Conclusion

Rural development forms an important agenda of the Government of India. The extent of budgetary allocation to the rural development sector is a witness to this fact. However, the uptake of e-governance in the rural development sector has been relatively slow. The main reasons for this are poor ICT infrastructure in rural areas, poor ICT awareness among agency officials working in rural areas and local language issues. Further, the remoteness of many of the RD agencies stifles re-engineering and integration efforts that form the basis of e-governance. The efforts are, however, on to extend infrastructure up to village level, but they are not made up to the satisfactory level. At the same time some of the States have gone ahead to provide connectivity up to Block level. This has helped in taking the e-governance efforts further closer to the people. Software applications are being implemented in some States at Block level. However, more needs to be done in terms of heralding e-governance in rural sector where most action takes place.

REFERENCES

Annual Report, (2002-03), Ministry of Rural Development, Government of India.

Hess, C.G. (2006), "Knowledge Management and Knowledge Systems for Rural Development", READER: GTZ Knowledge Management Available at http://www.fao.org/NR/com/gtzworkshop/Knowledge_Management_and_Systems.pdf.

Kapoor, Sapna and Gupta, Punam, "Self-employment: Single window help-line for entrepreneurs. Vol. 17, No. 1, Available at www17.ernat.in http://www.iimahd.ernat.in/egov/ifip/april 2007/apr2007.htm

Lightfoot, Clive and Scheuermeier, Ueli. (2006), "Linking Local Learners: Building knowledge management strategies for effective rural development in East Africa". Knowledge management strategies project with IFAD. Progress Report. Available at http://www.linkinglearners.net/downloads/RepKMSProgress.pdf.

Misra, D.C. and Dhingra, Anjali, (2001), "Rural Informatics Network for e-Governance in Rural Development", *Journal of Rural Development,* NIRD, Hyderabad.

Misra, D.C. *et al.* (2003), "E-KM Framework for Government organizations", *Information Systems Management,* Auerbach Publications, USA, Spring.

Rama Devi, T. (2006), "E-Learning tools and technologies for rural development community with special reference to training: Experiences of National Institute of Rural Development, ICT Conference on Digital Learning Environment, DRTC, Bangalore, 11th–13th January, 2006.

Wilson, D.S. (1996), "Managing Knowledge". Oxford Butterworth Heinemann in conjunction with the Institute of Management.

3

Perspective and Strategies of Knowledge Management in Dairy Cooperative Development

Samwel Kakuko Lopoyetum

Introduction : An Overview

Dairy sector provides ample employment opportunities to the people (communities) of both rural and urban areas. It plays a vital role in generation of regular income to the small and marginal farmers and downtrodden people living in rural areas to earn better livelihood. Dairying gives regular and steady income to dairy farmers next to agriculture and it is the best vocation to achieve higher growth of rural economy. Besides this, milk and milk products provides essential nutritious food to people (communities) of all walks of life. Dairy sector is facing large number of problems and hurdles in the current changing business environment, due to lack of Knowledge Management (KM). The liberalized economic environment has motivated Indian dairy cooperative industry to deal with competitive dairy trade and commerce (business). The flow of technological benefits and investment in dairy cooperative sector demands for the advance application of knowledge management in the dairy sector. Hence, the applications of knowledge management in dairy cooperative sector assume greater significance in crucial areas such as production of milk, procurement of milk, transportation (distribution), processing, marketing, management accounting system and financial management, etc. Information and communication technology is a vital component (organ) of knowledge based cooperative dairying productivity and sustainability in India. It is essential to ensure that the benefits of ICT and KM reach all socio-economic stratums of the rural dairy farmers in India. Village Knowledge Centre can provide crucial services to the rural dairy farmers by using advanced and modern information communication technology. Hence, setting up of VKCs to provide interactive sessions and also to the remote dairy villages will be a boon to the overall enhancement of rural industrialization and new technologies supported by appropriate input services and progressive public policies. It must lead to the second agricultural revolution and white revolution.

The KM and ICT revolutions allow for rapid growth in systematic assimilation, dissemination of relevant and timely information and access to universe of knowledge and communication through VKCs which will act as frontline delivery system to provide essential data and information required for the targeted population such as dairy farmers, ordinary farmers, and dairy specific farmers. Agriculture and Animal husbandry production in India *is dominated by resource and information poor farmers hence can get boost through VKCs and better agricultural dairy extension approach*. The setting up of information centre at villages with facilities using computer access to internet connection can offer reliable and upgraded multipurpose input services. It must be effective in the overall dissemination of the latest and need based information to dairy farmers. The ever changing economic environment is moving towards the era of *knowledge intensive dairy cooperative development*. This can be effectively done through Rural Knowledge Centres (RKCs) across the country. More than 70 per cent of India is rural and depend mainly on agriculture and dairy farming activities. But ICT led knowledge rural economy is absent or dismal. More than 6,00,000 villages can benefit from advanced KM and ICT technologies and make every village a knowledge centre to trigger *knowledge economy revolution in the rural areas*. Hence, pave way for the growth and development of dairy cooperative sector in the twenty-first century.

Knowledge has been defined by Davenport and Prusak (1998) as fluid mixture of experience, values, contextual information and Expert Insight that provides a framework for evaluation and incorporating new experiences and information. Knowledge comes from information processing by data and information. The dimension of Knowledge Management (KM) is highly important in dealing with dairy cooperative in developing countries such as India and Kenya. It helps in the expansion of dairy cooperative business organizations (dairy business, commerce and dairy industry) in the developing countries, they can gain advantage and effective working, sharing and re-using of knowledge for the purpose of developing dairy cooperative sector. The most important benefit of the Knowledge Management System (KMS) in the overall enhancement of the dairy firm's competitiveness while keeping costs at the minimum is extremely paramount, it improves the organizational responses, timely delivery of dairy products, goods and services into the open market/customer and act as an input to the promotion of research and development in developing countries such as in India and Kenya in the twenty-first century. It also gives an opportunity to add value for the information necessary for promoting dairy cooperative business organizations and overall dairy trade. It can provide data and knowledge basis to help the dairy farmer, marketing of milk, customers' service and technical supports. It can help in the overall dairy business organization in developing countries to be capable of solving their problems, guiding rightly and speedily, effectively and efficiently dealing with International Dairy Marketing. Knowledge Management may be viewed from Techno-Centric, organizational and combinatory point of views. These points of view are highly relevant in promoting dairy cooperative business organizations in developing countries, so that they can gain competitive advantage, which comes with faster learning and high chances of new knowledge creation, greater innovation, better customer experiences and increase the possibility of capturing Global Dairy Market in the twenty-first century. It enabled services, village call centres, dairy contact centres, transcription (data entry in VDKCs), hosting centres, computer hardware, software, cable TV in rural areas, satellite, suitable electronic communication requirements in rural areas to function effectively and efficiently under World Class Administration and Management of dairy cooperative business organizations. Moreover e-Governance of dairy cooperatives in developing countries assumes greater importance in the twenty-first century.

Knowledge management in dairy cooperative sector denotes getting the right knowledge from the right people, right time and helping people to share information, knowledge improve the organizational performance of dairy cooperative sector (Primary Milk Producers Societies, District Milk Producers Cooperative Union, State Level Milk Producers Cooperative Federation and National Level Milk Producers Federation). The knowledge management programme can be a tie-up with specific dairy organizational objective, goals, mission, visions for achieving the results, gain contact to competitive advantages, distributes knowledge, know-how, knowledge transfer, etc. Access to knowledge and positive impact effectiveness can be realized when individual feel enriched (with new ideas, solutions to problems) and are able to seek information at the time and place at where and when it is needed. In this context the development of Dairy information services kiosk is essential. It would provide details such as membership, society village, milk cattle, veterinary services; cattle feed services, day to day milk collections, and operations of the society, process society transactions. It can easily provide educational materials, process e-mail messages to and from members, societies, and union, upload data and information to union and they are all connected to the Internet Service Provider, Dairy Portal and server at the Union Level. Consequently, KM is extremely very significant in ensuring the growth and development of dairy cooperative sector in the new millennium. The dairy cooperative sector demands implementation of the effective and efficient Knowledge Management (KM) strategies and practices. This would depend on the improvement of the KM infrastructure and modernization of dairy cooperative into the twenty-first century. It would improve profitability, productivity, production, procurement, transportation processing, distributions, marketing and sales promotion in dairy cooperative marketing business organizations in the changing dairy business environment. It needs improved use and development of ICT and KM in dairy cooperative industry and would enable them in taking crucial commercial dairy decision making process in the changing dairy business environment. There must be favourable policy development and strategies for improving knowledge management in dairy cooperative sector in the twenty-first century.

Table 3.1 shows the production of milk by cooperatives in India. There are perceptible growths in all these areas.

Table 3.1: Production of Milk in India (1990-91 to 2004-05) ('000 tonnes)

Year	*Cow Milk*	*Buffalo Milk*	*Goat Milk*	*Total*
1990-91	22240(–)	28675(–)	2381(–)	53296(–)
1991-92	23038(3.50)	29600(3.13)	2348(-1.40)	55686(4.29)
1992-93	24291(5.15)	30846(4.04)	2515(6.64)	57962(3.93)
1993-94	25351(4.18)	32527(5.17)	2663(5.56)	60607(4.36)
1994-95	26122(2.95)	35637(8.63)	2749(3.13)	63805(5.02)
1995-96	26715(2.22)	35870(0.65)	2783(1.22)	66197(3.61)
1996-97	27916(4.30)	37541(4.45)	2898(3.97)	69145(4.26)
1997-98	29128(4.16)	38708(3.01)	3041(4.70)	72128(4.13)
1998-99	30454(4.35)	40413(4.22)	3236(6.02)	75424(4.37)
1999-00	32636(6.70)	42268(4.40)	3337(3.03)	78241(3.60)
2000-01	32967(1.00)	43428(2.67)	3266(–217)	80607(2.93)
2001-02	34516(4.50)	45402(4.35)	3501(6.71)	84406(4.50)
2002-03	34612(0.30)	46512(2.40)	3636(3.71)	86159(203)
2003-04	34973(0.01)	47979(3.05)	3708(1.94)	8802(2.18)
2004-05	36169(3.42)	49489(3.05)	3650(–1.60)	90733(2.92)

Source : Ministry of Statistics and Programme Implementation, Government of India.

Knowledge Management in Dairy Cooperative Business Organizations under Economic Liberalization and Globalized Environment

The scope and significance of Dairy Cooperative Business Organizations in the era of economic liberalization are portraying a mixed picture in the enhancement and proliferations of the socio-economic conditions of milk producers. In the era of economic liberalization, the milk production system, managerial economics, marketing functions and administrative functions of milk producers' cooperative societies must aim at ensuring effective and efficient working operations of the dairy cooperative business activities, thereby imparting the highest benefits to the dairy producers. It is imperative to ensure better practices and methods of prompt milk procurement, effective and efficient marketing operations, better pricing and distribution of milk and milk products in the local market areas, State, regional, national even capture reasonable share in the global dairy market KM and ICT can improve the working profile of the dairy cooperative system at all levels, such as the Primary Milk Producers Cooperative Societies, District Milk Producers Cooperative Union, State Level

Milk Producers Cooperative Federation as well as the National Dairy Cooperative Level Milk Federations.

Dairy farming system and milk production system is a subsidiary occupation and it can provide employment opportunities and livelihood to clarify farmers located in the rural and urban areas. As it can be perennial income source which can easily alleviate rural poverty problems to as greater extent in the present era of economic Liberalization and Globalization.

Tamil Nadu has a chequered history in dairy development. India's first cooperative dairy with processing facility was established in Madras city in 1925. At present there are 17 Milk Producer Cooperative Union (MPCU) in Tamil Nadu State and 10,665 Primary Milk Producer Cooperative Societies (PMPCS) which render reasonable services to their dairy members as well as the entire rural community by undertaking milk procurement operations, transportation, processing activities, sales and marketing business activities. As a matter of fact, it is highly imperative and essential in the era of economic liberalization and globalization to assess, whether the dairy cooperatives have made imprints in improving the overall socio-economic conditions of the rural masses particularly the weaker sections of the rural community. It is necessary to understand the contributions of dairy cooperatives marketing dimensions, and ultimately evolves a model for developing new generation dairy cooperative organizations to meet out the emerging challenges sprouting in the new economic environment brought about by liberalization, privatization and globalization.

In the era of Economic Liberalization, Privatization, Globalization and changing business environment it is highly essential to generate "generic" production and marketing strategies for the effective and efficient enhancement of the competitiveness of dairy cooperatives and dairy farmers. The benefits must be reflected in terms of their gainful, employment opportunities to dairy farmers and development of income generating dairy enterprises for the rural society.

Similarly, there must be immense scope in bringing forthwith suitable development strategies and practices for ensuring remunerative pricing policies for the dairy proceeds of small and marginal milk producers in tune with the changing business environment.

Consequently, there must be suitable KM strategies and measures for enhancing socio-economic development, empowerment, production and marketing benefits derived from dairy cooperative enterprises for the overall welfare development and growth of rural dairy enterprises and rural society in the changing business environment.

Impact of Knowledge Management and Spread Effects of Dairy Cooperatives in the Changing Business Environment

Dairy farming system in rural development is based on nature endowment and is considered to be land enterprises and gender neutral business enterprises in contrast with other types of resource production. It offers more favourable opportunity of employment and also provide constant source of income for rural dairy households. Moreover, it is scale neutral and spread all over the country (rural and urban). But, the unorganized dairy farmers were exploited at all levels. By all means by the unscrupulous elements usually the middlemen/vendors would ensure that they do not prosper or benefit from dairy enterprises. Since, the dairy farmers were milk producers, they were unable to overcome the problems associated with production, processing, selling and marketing of milk and milk products. Hence, with a view to encourage and develop modern dairying system as a dependable source of income among persons of small and medium size and as a subsidiary occupation providing gainful employment among dairy farming communities, cooperative privatization of dairying has been advocated from time to time. However, the functioning of cooperative dairy sector has been challenged by the new economic policies, new competitive practices, privatization, liberalization, and globalization. Hence, their role and scope must change with the changing times. They must use Knowledge Management and Knowledge Dairy Workers must emerge in the new millennium. The spread effects (multiplier effects) of dairy cooperative schemes are felt in terms of economic, social, empowerment, Education, Training, Sales, production, marketing and indirect benefits. In the current liberalized and globalized regime, it is necessary to gauge the growth, development dimensions, trend status, effect and impact of dairy cooperative sector in the changing business environment.

It is feared that, import of dairy products will dislodge the domestic market. The globalization process has created an environment leading to the fluctuation in price, marketing system, production system, etc., which adversely had an impact upon dairy products, milk production, and dairy cooperative sector. The tariff and non-tariff barriers and dairy world bodies are having bearing on the growth and development of dairy cooperative sector as a whole. In fact, on such dimension as the sanitary and phyto-sanitary measures have an impact on the export performance of dairy products and the performance of dairy cooperative sector. Hence, there is imperative need to understand the effect and impact of liberalization on dairy cooperative sector in the changing global scenario and application of Knowledge Management in dairy cooperative business organizations.

Impact of Knowledge Management in Dairy Cooperatives

It refers to the material and non-material KM effects; it also refers to the impact of Knowledge Management on the values and principles guiding constitution, management and operation of cooperatives which together result in or enabled developments in the socio-economic conditions of dairy farmers, production, marketing of members produce and non-members. It also deals and concerned with the improvement in the existing state of affairs as felt by milk producers as a test of impact and effect of Knowledge Management in dairy cooperatives. In the changing business environment it is essential to eventually move towards formulating a model for *New Generation Dairy Cooperative System* at grassroot level to cope up with the negative impact of economic liberalization, privatization and globalization. This can be made possible with the application of Knowledge Management in dairy cooperatives.

Knowledge Management and Socio-Economic Impact

The socio-economic impact of dairy cooperatives can be directly, felt at the level of members and non-members in respect of changes in awareness, realization of social, democratic and empowerment benefits of dairy cooperatives, creation of a sense of security and ownership in the dairy cooperative business organizations. Moreover, the economic impact of dairy cooperatives refers to multiplying of houses, acquiring lands derived from the income of the dairy cooperatives, investments, enlargement of livestock units, increased bank balances, will be the impact and effect on dairy cooperatives at the individual level of the dairy farmers. It will also be reflected at the dairy cooperative organizational levels, which in turn are applying Knowledge Management practices, strategies and theories from time to time.

Knowledge Management Marketing Benefits in Changing Environment

The marketing benefits can be felt when dairy farmers supply milk to the society without interruption, interception and eventually collection of money (milk proceeds) without delay. KM is the support system of these operations. The services availed to improve the quality of milk and the derived marketing benefits at the individual levels are highly imperative and significant in marketing milk products and its operations in dairy cooperative business organizations. It must be undertaken in the most effective and efficient manner in the changing environment, as a result of the use and application of the Knowledge Management.

The New Millennium Dimensions of Knowledge Management of Dairy Cooperatives

The dimension of Knowledge Management in dairy cooperatives can be felt and understood in the following dimensions, viz.:

(i) Social Dimension

- Education and Training.
- Change in Family Size and household.
- Create awareness among neighbours and other cooperatives.
- Exposure to mass media.
- Frequent Contact with change agents (social and economic).
- Complete Social participation involvement in the Knowledge Management areas.

(ii) Economic Dimension

- Total assets improvement.
- Family income improvement.
- Occupational professionalism and perfectionism.
- Change in size of landholding and economic benefits.

(iii) Cooperation Appraisal Dimension

- Duration of membership enhancement.
- Proportion of borrowings from Cooperatives can be determined through Knowledge Management.
- Knowledge on cooperation and its usefulness are enhanced.
- Complete participation in cooperative management and administration.
- Services availed by dairy farmers from dairy cooperatives are expanded and professionalized.

(iv) Dairy Cooperative Dimensions

- Area under Dairy farming system can be expanded and modernized.
- Cattle population and livestock breeding system enhanced.
- Type of fodder and feeds are diversified.
- Age of dairy cattle can be determined and assessed.
- High quality production of dairy milk and milk products.
- Dairy products are diversified.
- Income from dairy milk animals are enhanced from time to time.

(v) Constitution of Dairy Cooperatives

- Membership coverage are enhanced.
- Coverage of weaker sections are made possible.

(vi) Benefits and Management of Dairy Cooperatives

- Democratic benefits.

- Leadership change.
- Empowerment benefits.
- Management efficiency.
- Professional management.
- Promotion of legal system and legislation.

(vii) Business of Dairy Cooperatives

- Service mix.
- Economic viability.
- Sustainable development.
- Marketing and production benefits.

(viii) Production of Dairy Cooperatives

- Scope of better production enhancement.
- Productivity enhancement.
- Education and training.
- Enhancement of production and supply of inputs (backward integration).

(ix) Marketing of Dairy Cooperatives

- High quality of dairy products and services.
- Pricing system is better.
- Promotional activities are enhanced.

Knowledge Management in Dairy Cooperatives Today and Tomorrow

Today, dairy cooperatives play a pivotal role in the rural economy in general and provision of gainful employment opportunities in the rural areas in particular. Dairy cooperatives have made commendable socio-economic impact on the country over the years. In fact, several studies have evaluated the growth, progress and development of dairy cooperatives in the context of their commercial aspects, measuring their efficiency with the yardsticks of the volume of the business and profit content of the business. It is essential to understand the socio-economic aspects of dairy farmers, Knowledge Management in dairy cooperatives, production and marketing operations undertaken by dairy farmers, the dairy milk producers union, primary milk producer cooperative society and impact of dairy cooperatives from the perception of members and non-members under the liberalized era. Hence, keeping all these aspects in view, a few questions need to be clarified today and tomorrow; they are: Do members of dairy cooperative realize socio-economic and marketing benefits of dairy cooperatives with the help of Knowledge Management? Do the dairy cooperatives create awareness dynamism among members and non-members juxtaposition the KM liberalization and globalization perspectives? What is the perception of members and non-members towards the social, economic, empowerment, production and market benefits of dairy cooperatives in the liberalized regime? Whether application of Knowledge Management would be enabled for stable democratic governance, e-governance or not? Whether the Knowledge Management enabled them, under liberalization scenario then to be vibrant economic units or not? Whether dairy cooperatives acquired necessary strength and support to serve better their community through Knowledge Management? Do the dairy cooperatives have ability to withstand themselves amidst competitive forces in the context of the application of Knowledge Management and changed economics policies and business environment? What do they suggest to draw a line between limits and Knowledge Management in delimits of liberalization on dairy cooperatives? All these factors/issues and relevant parameters, indicators, issues on liberalization and Knowledge Management on dairy cooperative sectors are to be addressed in the present changing dairy business environment.

The essential salient features and paradigms of Knowledge Management in dairy cooperative sector in the changing business environments are :

- It must provide positive impact of its operations to facilitate the dairy cooperatives to provide greater management and democratic control benefits to members of dairy cooperative society in the long run.
- The effects of Knowledge Management must provide significant empowerment benefits on dairy cooperatives and its members.

- The impact of Knowledge Management must enhance managerial efficiency, production and marketing efficiency of dairy cooperatives business organizations.
- The impact of Knowledge Management must provide the dairy cooperatives with a strong base for productivity, profitability and sustainable development of dairy industry in the changing business environment.
- The impact of Knowledge Management must significantly provide ways and means for the cost competitiveness and cost minimization in the dairy cooperative business organizations.
- The impact of Knowledge Management must provide the best technical inputs, value addition and diversification of dairy cooperatives in the changing business environment.
- The impact and effect of Knowledge Management on dairy cooperative sector can be felt in terms of social, economic, empowerment, production, processing, marketing benefits, and indirect benefits by the cooperative dairy unions, PMCS among the members and non-members of dairy cooperatives in the liberalized and globalized business environment.

There is an inherent need of ensuring and making paradigm shift in the prosperity and posterity of dairy farmers through Knowledge Management in the changing environment. It will help the rural people and milk producers increase their milk production particularly the small and marginal milk producers. In the liberalized environment, dairy cooperative societies are expected to compete with private dairy business organizations, therefore, needs competitive strategies. It is essential to generate "generic" production and marketing strategies for the enhancement of the competitiveness of dairy cooperatives and farmers through application of Knowledge Management in the new millennium.

In the new environment there is immense scope in bringing forthwith suitable strategies for ensuring remunerative pricing policies for the dairy proceeds of small and marginal milk producers and creating awareness through Knowledge Management (creation, communication, application, experience, new capabilities, superior performance, innovation, expertise, dissemination, right time, acquisition, re-use of knowledge....)

Moreover, there is imperative need to apply Knowledge Management and bring out suitable strategies and measures for enhancing socio-economic development, empowerment production and marketing benefits derived from dairy cooperative enterprises for the overall welfare development and growth of rural dairy farmers.

As a matter of policy option there must be crucial and critical considerations in reviewing and assessing the impact of Knowledge Management and liberalization of dairy cooperative sector in terms of materials and non-materials dimensions. It should also determine the benefits and non-benefits of Knowledge Management and economic liberalization on the entire gamut of dairy cooperatives business organizations. Next, it is essential to assess the efficiency of dairy cooperative organizations and take suitable policy decisions on their improvement and strengthening in the long run in the light of Knowledge Management and ICT. We must look for better ways and means of enhancing strategies of development of dairy cooperative sector to attain higher profitability, productivity, economic viability, and sustainability under the globalized regime and new economic environment.

Impact of Knowledge Management, Economic Liberalization and Globalization on Dairy Cooperative Business Organizations

- The above mentioned details are given in Chart 3.1.

The Relevance and Strategies of Knowledge Management in Dairy Cooperative Sector

Dairy Cooperative sector is facing large number of problems and hurdles in the current changing business environment, due to lack of knowledge management (KM). The liberalized economic environment has motivated Indian dairy cooperative industry to deal with dairy trade and commerce (business). The flow of technological benefits and investment in dairy cooperative sector demands for the advance application of knowledge management in the dairy sector. Hence, the applications of knowledge management in the dairy sector assume greater significance in crucial areas such as production of milk, procurement of milk,

Chart 3.1: Impact of Knowledge Management, Economic Liberalization and Globalization on Dairy Cooperative Business Organizations

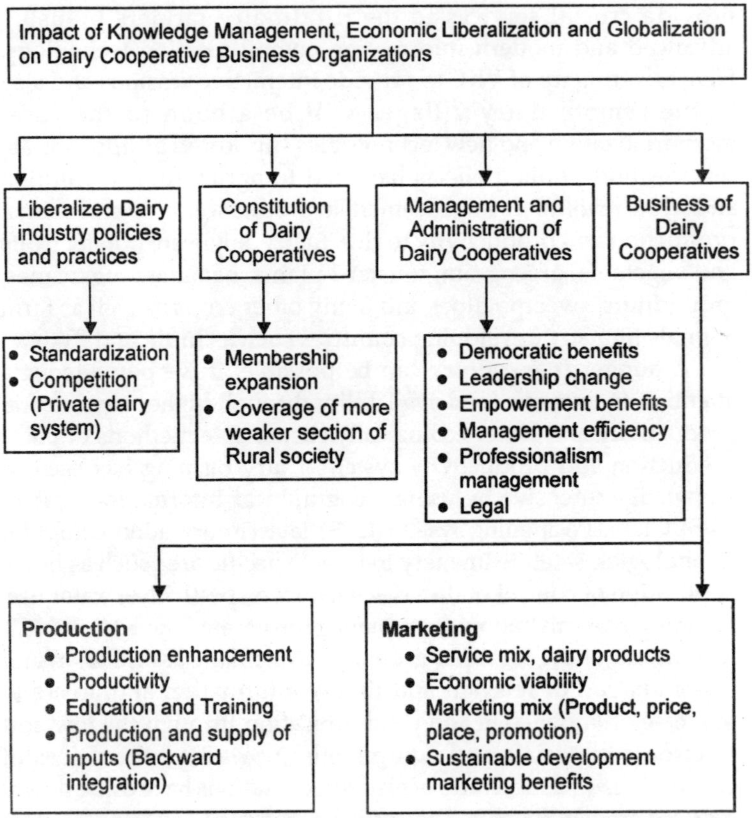

Source: Conceptual Model generated by Dr. Samwel Kakuko Lopoyetum (2006) GRU; paper presented at national level seminar on Knowledge Management, Indira Gandhi Women's College, Trichy.

transportation (distribution), processing, marketing, management accounting system and financial management, etc.

Knowledge Management and Village Knowledge Centres (VKCs) for Dairy Cooperative Development

Information and communication technology is a vital component of knowledge based cooperative dairy productivity in India. It is essential to ensure that the direct and indirect benefits of ICT reach all the socio-economic stratum of the rural dairy farmers throughout the country. Village Knowledge Centres (VKCs) can provide crucial services to the rural dairy farmers by using advanced and modern information communication technology. Hence, setting up of VKC to provide interactive sessions and also to the remote dairy villages will be a boon to the rural industrialization and new technologies supported by appropriate services and public policies have led to agricultural revolution and white revolution, improvement in production, crop and animal production and productivity to rice, maize, soybean, potato, fruits and vegetable, greengram, mustard plants, bananas, sugarcanes, groundnuts, sweetpotatoes and many other crops as well as farm animals in many developing countries such as India and Kenya.

A hunger free country can be possible, if we pay adequate attention to improve food availability through higher agricultural productivity and better ecologically sustainable methods of dairy production and productivity system, Dairy farming has become knowledge intensive by using Geographical Information System (GIS), Global Positioning System (GPS), latest information, computer technologies, satellite imagery to target specific area such as in the application of control of diseases, fertilizers, pesticides, water use, planning administration, farm management, etc. The KM and ICT revolutions allow for rapid growth in systematic assimilation and dissemination of relevant and timely information and access to universe of knowledge and communication through the low cost electronic materials and equipments (nowadays the prices of electronic gadgets and rates of electronic taxations have come down/ reduced tremendously). The software industry is providing new tools to increase animal productivity and create new opportunities for understanding even complexities of dairy cooperative industry, agro industrial system, intensive agriculture etc. Knowledge Connectivity to dairy villages through VKCs will act as frontline delivery stem to provide essential data and information required for the targeted population such as dairy farmers ordinary farmers, dairy specific farmers, fishermen, craftsmen, rural artisans and traders, business men, unemployed youth, health and overall rural development. Application of technology for improving animal productivity is necessary in rural areas, particularly in the changing business and economic environment.

Knowledge Management (KM) in Agricultural and Animal Production (Husbandry) : Linking the Missing Link through VKCs

There is direct link between Agricultural Development and dairy cooperative development. KM can be created and shared by these two important components of Rural Economic Growth and Development. The typical knowledge required in agricultural production extent to soil science and management seeds, water management, pre-harvesting practices, agronomic practices and post-harvesting management, productivity increase, banking, financial assistance, technical assistance to farmers, meteorological forecasting for disaster warning, etc. VKCs can use advanced technology and can promote technology for sustainable development and create knowledge society. Agriculture and Animal Husbandry Production in India is dominated by resource and information poor farmers hence can get boost through VKCs and better agricultural and dairy extension approach. The setting up of information centre at village with facilities using computer access to internet connection can offer reliable and upgraded multipurpose input service. It must be opt for an effective dissemination of the latest and need based information to dairy farmers. It is heartening that M.S. Swaminathan Research Foundation (MSSRF) had initiated VKC in Pondicherry in 1988 to provide rural families access to various information fostering agricultural and rural development through the use of ICT. The content of dissemination prepared using indigenous knowledge with generic information including those propounded by the subject matter specialist and use of multimedia interactive system.

The changing environment is moving towards the era of knowledge intensive dairy cooperative development and agricultural development. This can be effectively done through Rural Knowledge Centres (RKC) across the country. More than 70 per cent of India is rural and depend mainly on agriculture and dairy farming activities, but ICT led knowledge rural economy is absent or dismal. Therefore, they must be brought under VKCs. More than 6,00,000 villages can benefit from advanced ICT technologies and make every village a knowledge centre to trigger knowledge economy revolution in the rural areas in the new millennium. Hence, pave way for the growth and development of dairy cooperative sector in the twenty-first century.

Genesis of Village Knowledge Centres (VKCs)

Village Knowledge Centre (VKC) was earlier initiated in Pondicherry by M.S. Swaminathan Research Foundation (MSSRF) in 1998 and thereafter many other States in India adopted it. It focused on various informations fostering agricultural and overall rural development issues with the help of Information and Communication Technology (ICT). It created the idea of evolving the Value Addition Centre (VAC), sub-station at Villanur Pondicherry connecting to ten village knowledge centres through a hybrid wireless network comprising of computers, telephones, VHF duplex radio devices and facilitating both voice and data transfer. Local volunteers, mostly women, gather the information and feed in into the internet by using indigenous knowledge with generic information including those propounded by the Subject Matter Specialist (SMS) and use of Multimedia Interactive System (MIS). The VAC is done for VKC by preparing it in the local language (Tamil). It has generated a number of databases to answer the queries of the local people's day-to-day requirement. The advertisements and informations are published in the media as rural yellow pages. The facilitator was given adequate Education and Training and providing a token incentive of Re. 1 per visitor to the centre. This initiative paved way for the growth and development of Village Knowledge Centres.

Accelerating Growth of Village Dairy Knowledge Centres (VDKCs)

In the context of globalization and new economic scenario, the villagers (dairy farmers) are required to understand and enhance their animal productivity, reduce production cost, get higher price, marketing of the produce/commodity in a competitive manner. They must improve the quality of their dairy produce/ commodities. As a pre-requisite they must understand details such as genetic (i.e., farm products), legal (their Rights), quality (i.e., sanitary and phytosanitary measures) and commerce, business, trade (i.e., local prices and external markets) to become more competitive in the new millennium. Village Dairy Knowledge Centres (VDKCs) play a significant role to measure and dispense local information on good governance of dairy cooperative societies, e-governance entitlement and state of the art infrastructure or world class infrastructure, accessing to dynamic relevant information on weather, dairy markets, prices, products promotion and online public services, etc. It is essential to promote knowledge centres in more than 6,00,000 villages by 2010. Moreover, it must mobilize partnership among the public and private sectors, academicians and professionals, mass media and civil society organizations to accelerate the growth and development of Village Dairy Knowledge Centres (VDKCs).

Objectives of Village Dairy Knowledge Centres (VDKCs)

The major objectives are mainly to provide information and data and promote communication process particularly those which are required and relevant to the dairy and animal production (Husbandry) information system. The objectives are :

- To disseminate information directly to the rural dairy farmers at the grassroot level/micro level. This can be done through the PMPCs.
- To predict the rainfall and encourage water harvesting technologies during rainy seasons for production of fodder and fodder crops.
- To bring access to a range of information of services relating to animal production and agricultural growth, production cost, demand, supply, marketing and how to increase productivity (animal and crops).
- To disseminate market information system to the rural dairy farmers, the marketing requirements of their milk products or demand and supply caused by changing Economic Environment.
- To know the consumers requirements and meet their needs and wants on time.
- To provide information and knowledge to the dairy farmers on the availability of cattle feeds veterinary services, fertilizers, pesticides and other animal

husbandry/agricultural requisite including adoption of New Dairy Technologies Development and Agricultural Technologies brought about by Technological changes in the new economic environment. Dairy husbandry is directly linked to the development of agriculture. Hence, imperative to develop and provide information to dairy farmers about agricultural development.

- To promote the rural information infrastructures by developing highly developed rural Communication Technology and Knowledge Management Infrastructure.

Consequently, In the changing economic environment, the Village Dairy Knowledge Centres are essential to facilitate the flow of dairy inputs, services and products in the global markets in a more efficient and effective manner. Since the market is growing global, the rural dairy farmers may be required to increase their animal productivity by adopting newly advanced technology and method of production and can be possible through the setting up of Village Dairy Knowledge Centres. The Village Dairy Knowledge Centre will provide information knowledge and communication to the dairy farm men and women which require dynamic information relating to dairy farm management, meteorological and market factors related to areas such as agro-forestry, agro-processing, crops and animal husbandry, etc. VDKCs can help to provide economic, social and cultural opportunities to all classes of people living in the rural areas. It should provide essential data and information requirement for taking decisions by the dairy farmers, by understanding their own requirements and identify their core competencies and VDKCs can empower the youth to upgrade the level of dairy development activities for their villages such as establishing rural dairy enterprise which will facilitate large scale employment.

There is a possibility of developing *PURA dairy enterprises* to take advantage of the PURA Programmes/Schemes. The government should improve e-infrastructures in village areas through its National e-Governance plan. Through VDKCs, it can emphasize on rural ICT initiatives to non-formal, on-degree learning, etc. The VDKCs can be powerful instrument or tool in concern of right to information (at the correct time and place), content creation and capacity building in the rural areas (Micro-level ICT strategies) to promote growth and development of Dairy Cooperative sector in the new millennium.

Dimension of Village Dairy Knowledge Centres (VDKCs)

The scope and dimensions of VDKCs can be understood in terms of viz. :

1. VDKCs can efficiently enhance the procurement, transportations, processing marketing, distribution of the milk and milk products/commodities from rural to urban, to national and globalized dairy market environment.
2. The emergence of VDKCs and info-kiosk movement can be promoted by NGOs and corporate (private) sector, the local Panchayats and SHGs can access the scientific and technical knowledge, to solve the local emerging problem with greater care. This has been done by Indian Tobacco Company (ITC), Godrej company, Technomind, etc., in some small scale manner, hence, this approach needs enlargement of scope and dimensions in the changing economic environment.
3. Through National Digital Gateway for rural livelihood security, it can monitor the climate changes to farmers which can take effective decision by dairy farmers regarding the flush and lean seasons. This is very important due to the Global Warming problems caused by the Green House Gas (GHG) emission which cause negative effect on environment, ecology and economy.
4. The Rural ICT network through the VDKCs helps the dairy farming system viability, sustainability and scalability of the rural knowledge revolution to improve the lives of the rural dairy families.
5. It helps to know the feasibility of market potential in the dairy trade movement and Agri-business Management.
6. It creates sustainable rural micro-enterprises in the area of dairy farming, agri business, agro-forestry, agro-industry, fisheries, handicrafts, animal husbandry, poultry farms, expansion of rural dairy farms, etc.
7. It helps not only to improve the dairy farmer's knowledge regarding the Animal Husbandry Management but also

the knowledge of the current dairy industry affairs and present conditions of the economy in the changing economic environment and global dairy scenario.

8. It also provides a vision to dairy farmers to develop their future generations who shall be treated as Techno Savvy and ICT enabled generations can improve and enhance animal productivity and animal husbandry practices.
9. There is a chance to develop a new economic strategy by the illiterate farmers to become literate through VDKCs. Due to this, the Village Dairy Knowledge Centre is vital to the dairy farmer living conditions in the rural areas.
10. It will lead to *a new 100 per cent Literate country,* if used properly and adequately by the rural dairy farmers.
11. It is also an influencing factor to make India become a developed country by 2020. At the same time, become knowledge economy with knowledge workers deployed in the Animal Production field and Agricultural Development sector.
12. It helps to gain higher living standard of the rural dairy farmers and the entire socio-economic development of the people (community) in the rural areas is motivated through setting up the most effective and efficient VDKCs.

Constraints of VDKCs

Crucial obstacles to these initiatives are :

- Lack of local/non-availability of global content in their regional languages,
- Physical (e.g. electricity and other electronic equipments) and financial problems in the permanent establishment and maintenance of village dairy knowledge level kiosks,
- Lack of organizational and institutional structures for developing the VDKCs,
- Insufficient network between institutions in information management and administration,
- Poor policies/strategies to formulate a world class road map for harnessing such ICTs initiatives by addressing the VDKCs constraints faced by the institutions and government agencies,

- Inadequate proactive role both in network, content development and transfer, adoption, diffusion and absorption of technology (Roger's Diffusion Innovation Process),
- Deficiency of public investment in VDKCs to promote, dairy cooperative development, milk production and marketing. This has direct impact and effect on animal productivity and animal husbandry in the long run, and
- Predominance of marginal and small holdings dairy farmers in the rural areas can be an obstacle, because they are enormously scattered in several Agro-ecological and Agro-economic Zones.

Organizations which are Responsible for Effective Implementation of Village Knowledge Centres

Many organizations can take up VDKCs, such as Self–Help Groups (SHGs), Non-Government Organizations (NGO), District Administration, Village Panchayats, CAPART, Local Communities, MSSRF, Agricultural Cooperative Marketing Organisations, NNDB, Dairy Cooperative Unions, NCDC, NCUI, etc.

Because of the population explosion taking place in the country, the food and nutritional security is very crucial. In spite of the urgent population needs and requirements there is urgent need to double or triple food production by all means. The problem of huge national demand, limited natural resources, and regional imbalances and political constraints, the dairy development problems, livestock development problems, agricultural growth, production, periodicity and development can be mitigated through the knowledge centres. Sometimes, the natural disaster have directly affected the Indian agriculture and its allied sectors, but still it is performing well as compared to other sectors because of the efforts taken by the government and research institutions/ organizations such as ICAR through knowledge centres.

Now, we have to struggle to enhance prosperity, productivity and gain higher achievement and growth in dairy development and agricultural field, more land brought under cultivation, irrigation, Advance Research and Development (R&D) in dairy sector, dairy processing, export, etc., can be attained by linking with dairy cooperative societies through VDKCs. Here, the cooperative sector has exclusively offered its unchallengeable functionaries and direct investment to promote growth and prosperity of dairy cooperative sector. Also, we have to introduce new varieties of animal's crop, fruits, cereals through large-scale production of hybridization process of animal breeding and scientific research carried out by the well-established Agricultural and Animal Husbandry Research Stations in India and also through Agricultural Cooperative Organizations/institutions.

The fast moving world economy towards establishment of a competitive open market economy within countries and in between countries has changed the operations and status of dairy cooperative sector in India. In this competitive new millennium, the dairy cooperative sector should attempt to develop new cooperative approach by linking with VDKCs in order to enhance the growth production, productivity and development of dairy industrial sector. There is an urgent need for evolving new dairy cooperative approach and New Generation Dairy Cooperative perspective though VDKCs, i.e., by starting and initiating new generation cooperative organizations using ICT in order to enhance prosperity, growth, production, productivity and overall dairy production and improve development of the socio-economic livelihood of the farmers and at the same time make dairy cooperative sector more sustainable, more productive and more profitable more competitive in the Twenty First Century. All these can be made possible through effective and efficient linkage operations of VDKCs at the grass root with apex national level federations like, NCUI, NAFED, TRIFED, NCDC, NDDB, BDDF, IFFCO, KRIBCHO and also link them with the agencies of the Government of India at the grass root level. In the changing economic and dairy business scenario, there is greater demand for information for making crucial dairy farm management decisions on time. But inadequate access to immediate and relevant dairy information is being felt as one of the major constraints at the grass root level/micro-level. Hence, the application of Micro level KM strategies and practices which are highly imperative in the new millennium is needed.

Need for New Development Policy for Strengthening and Accelerating VKDC

KM and ICT network is very much essential to undertake dairy production, increase agricultural growth, development and increasing productivity. KM and ICT is still very poor in rural areas which face difficulties to sell their products in the global markets. It can support bottom-up articulation of dairy development needs and perceptions of dairy farmers (micro level approach in KM and ICT in dairy cooperative sector, growth, production and productivity is the need of the hour). It comprises of various developing techniques and infrastructure for storage, processing, distributions, marketing and management of information, upgradation of knowledge, skills, changing the attitude of rural dairy farmers, keeping information security, etc. Therefore, there is imperative need for the development of new dairy cooperative development policy for strengthening and accelerating Village Dairy Knowledge Centres in the present changing economic environment.

Dairy Cooperative Development and Application of Knowledge Management in Milk Producers Federations

The Tamil Nadu Cooperative Milk Producers Federation Limited is an apex body of 17 Districts Cooperative Milk Producers Unions; the Primary Milk Producers Cooperative Societies are 9,012. In the livestock and poultry census (1997) stated that in Tamil Nadu, the total cattle population was 93.63 lakhs which accounts for 35.8 per cent of the total livestock population in the country and buffalo population was 27.17 lakhs which accounts for 10.39 of the total livestock population. The cattle population, which was 105.72 lakhs in 1974, has got reduced to 93.63 lakhs in 1997. Similarly, the buffalo population, which was 28.53 lakhs reduced to 27.16 lakhs during the same period.

However, the milk production in Tamil Nadu has increased tremendously over the past 20 years. From only, 1.74 millions tonnes in 1981, it has risen to 5 million tonnes in 2001. This has resulted an increase in per capita availability of milk to 219 gm per day, which is very close to the ICMR recommendations of 220 gm per day. With the present trend, it is hoped that the ICMR recommendations will be reached shortly. This is purely due to the breeding policy adopted in Tamil Nadu, which is in tune with the national policy. In this scenario, knowledge management is highly useful and applicable at milk producers federation level to deal with dairy cooperative development at the State level.

Knowledge management in dairy cooperative sector denotes getting the right knowledge from the right people, right time and helping people to share information knowledge and improve the organizational performance of dairy cooperative sector (Primary Milk Producers Societies, District Milk Producers Union, State Level Milk Producers Federations and National Level Milk Producers Federations). The knowledge management programme can be tied up with specific dairy organizational objectives, goals, mission, visions, to achieve target results, gain contact to competitive advantages, distribute knowledge, know-how, knowledge transfer, etc., hence, at milk producers federations level, they can apply KM in all the functional area of management.

Tamil Nadu is an agriculture-oriented State and majority of the dairy farmers, agricultural labourers own livestock. Dairy sector provides ample employment opportunities to the people of both rural and urban areas, therefore, Knowledge Management is highly needed for them. It plays a vital role in generation of regular income to the small and marginal farmers and downtrodden people living in rural areas to earn better livelihood. Dairying gives regular and steady income to the dairy farmers next to agriculture and it is the best vocation to achieve higher growth of rural economy. Besides this, milk and milk products provide essential nutritional food requirement to the people of all walks of life.

In the wake of liberalization policy, private dairies have also entered into the field of dairying. High priority has been given for improving the performance of milk cooperatives by adopting a systematic approach and proper strategy in Milk Cooperatives. Significant achievement has been made by Milk Producers Cooperative Societies, Unions and Federations in the State of Tamil Nadu, therefore it is highest time to use Knowledge Management strategies and practices to strengthen accelerate the growth and development of dairy cooperative sector in the changing economic environment.

Keeping these objectives in mind, a large number of activities are undertaken by the Dairy Development Department, viz., provision of free veterinary health cover to all animals owned by the members of milk cooperatives, implementation of artificial insemination programme, supply of balanced cattle feed and to impart training and education to farmers about the modern animal husbandry methods and practices. This can be made possible with the use of Knowledge Management strategies and methods.

All activities, which are essential for the upgradation of the milch animals and improving their productivity in the long run, can be popularized with the use of Knowledge Management System.

Provisions of necessary infrastructure facilities for marketing milk and milk products and supply of quality milk to the consumers can be made by way of establishing new chilling centres, pasteurization plants and adoption of modern processing system. Awareness can be created among the milk producers to utilize these infrastructural facilities located in various places in the regions.

Knowledge Management at the Primary Milk Producers Cooperative Society Producers and Consumers Awareness

Most of the rural people especially women do eke out their livelihood by rearing milk animals (2-5 animals) and supplying milk to the Milk Cooperative Societies. Keeping this in view and to improve the rural economy and enhance the personal income of the stakeholders in rural areas, Government directed the Tamil Nadu Cooperative Milk Producers Federation Limited, and District Cooperative Milk Producers Unions to raise the procurement price of the cow milk from Rs. 9.50 to Rs. 10.50 per litre and buffalo milk from Rs. 11.44 to Rs. 12.50 per litre with effect from 1.6.2004 and that the milk cost as per the revised procurement price should be disbursed to the Milk Producers without any further delay. While increasing the procurement price of that milk it is assured that there would not be any increase in the selling price to the consumers. Hence, KM can be useful in creating awareness and popularize the schemes and programmes of government which are initiated from time to time.

The average milk procurement in the State through cooperative societies has been increasing from 18.88 per cent, which shows an annual growth of 9.11 per cent. In order to ensure better price to members and procurement of high quality milk, the system of testing of milk was introduced at primary cooperative societies level. The steps taken to improve the quality of milk have yielded good results. The quality of milk received at Chennai with regard to fat had increased from 4.3 to 4.5 per cent and the SNF (Solid Non Fat) in the milk increased from 8.2 to 8.3 per cent. As a result of these improvements, better quality of milk is supplied to consumers. The consumer awareness can be created with the help of Knowledge Management Systems.

Pursuant to the efforts taken by the Milk Producers Federation and District Producers Cooperative Unions in clearing the dues, payment of dues to the milk producers have been settled fully in the previous financial years and it is being maintained in the current year also. Now the milk cost payment is made to the milk producers once in 10 days without any further backlog. The Anand pattern model advocate for the prompt payment of milk proceeds to the dairy producers.

To extend the financial benefits such as payment of milk cost in time, payment of bonus and "patronage rebate" to the milk pouring members of the Primary Milk Producers Cooperative Societies, it is mandatory that every dairy cooperative society has to function on profit. Keeping this in mind, effective steps have been taken to improve the financial conditions of the dairy cooperative societies and as a result of such effective measures all the 7,117 functioning societies are working on profit in the current competitive dairy environment. The District Cooperative Milk Producers Unions at Salem, Madurai, Coimbatore, Trichy, Erode, Sivaganga, Tirunelveli and the Nilgiris have adopted Common Mnemonic Symbol, which symbolize the supply of quality milk to the consumers. This has paved the way for popularizing the brand "*Aavin*" among the public. In this way, the KM system can link both the producers and consumers in the present changing competitive business environment.

Access to Knowledge Management by Members of the Dairy Cooperatives

Access to knowledge impact effectiveness when individual feels enriched (with new ideas, solutions to problems) and is able to seek information at the time and place where it is needed. Individuals need to trust the information before the distilled knowledge is applied to a specific action. KM project can at best hope to create large electronic networks which will then support the emergence of human networks keen to consult each other and begin to value and trust the information/knowledge that is pooled and disseminated. Knowledge management initiatives should supplement traditional networking through face to face contact, rather than supplant such initiatives.

Another way of capturing indigenous innovations by organizing various walks of teams of volunteers through clusters of villages to learn about and document all rural innovations. The documents are then widely disseminated through print and digital media. The Community radios, educational TV and broadcasting may have a very useful role in building and empowering rural dairy farming communities. When rural women learnt to video tape the poor progress of rural projects in Kenya and showed the clippings to decision makers in far away cities, the response was quick and positive. This can be possible in dairy cooperative sector in India and Kenya.

Public cooperatives and private partnership is likely to play a very important role in the changing environment, cooperative entrepreneurship approach is needed to create demand for knowledge and information amongst the rural population. A creation of a large number of access points for electronic services requires large investments, managerial competence and innovations. Private partners can bring the necessary funds and innovative energy to create the infrastructure and keep it viable over time. The mind-set within implementing and government agencies needs to change in order to encourage partnership by structuring agreements that provide for a fair return on investments by the private partners, they can bring the necessary expertise and innovative strategies to create better working performing dairy cooperative business organisations. The mind-set within implementing and government agencies needs to change to encourage partnership by structuring agreements that provide for a fair return on investments by the private partner but any type of profiteering can be regulated through cooperative approach.

Making the content of KM appropriate to local rural dairy communities will require a decentralized approach to content development and micro-level application system. Some of the existing institutions that serve rural clientele such as extension workers, dairy leader, and handloom cooperatives can play a significant role in developing content, provided, that internet is ubiquitous enough to deliver this content to the rural dairy producers population in the long run.

Significance of Dimensions of Dairy Information Management Services Kiosk

With the initiatives of National Dairy Development Board (NDDB) out of 70,000 dairy cooperative societies in the country around 26,000 are using Electronic Milko Testers (EMT) and around 2,500 are using the PC connected electronic milko tester machines (known as Automatic Milk Collection System). These systems introduced have pave way for very satisfactory milk collection methods and facilitated immediate payment to dairy farmer based on the quality and quantity of milk delivered. The success of these systems coupled with inexpensive connectivity, opportunity offered by internet, motivated the CEG–IIMA to enhance the PC at the automatic Milk Collection System (AMCS) into a Dairy Information Services Kiosk (DISK) and offer an extensive knowledge and service delivery mechanism through a dairy portal. The DISK when used with dairy portal of the union enhances the scope of services that would benefit the farmers as well as the dairy industry. The development of dairy information services Kiosk is essential it would provide details such as membership dairy society village, milch cattle, veterinary services, cattle feed services, day to day milk collections and operations of the society, process society transactions, educational material, e-mail messages to and from members, society, union, upload data to union and they all connected to the internet service provider, dairy portal and server at the union level. Hence, KM is a fulcrum of dairy cooperative development in the present economic environment.

Instances of Development of Dairy Portal and Application in Dairy Industry

The dairy portal is designed to provide an interactive dairy information and education channel to the members of the DCS and others in the dairy sector. To a large extent, the contents are created and the interaction is facilitated in the regional language as well as English. A toggle button on the main page of the portal facilitates switching between these two languages. The portal can be accessed through internet browser by any authorized user on the internet system.

The dairy portal has textual as well as multimedia content useful to the dairy farmers, extension workers, business executives and researchers dealing with the dairy sector. The portal mainly offers services such as education, entertainment, discussion forum, frequently asked questions, data transfers, application forms for submission to various agencies, e-commerce, and e-banking.

On the educational front, the portal typically holds the data on best practices in breeding and rearing milch cattle, feeding and keeping animal healthy, producing high quality milk, care to be taken in buying and selling the cattle and several other aspects to educate and advise the users. In addition, the portal gives hyper links to other rural education website. For example, the prototype portal has provided hyper link to SRISTI (an NGO working with IIMA) which has documented thousands of rural innovations in multimedia format.

On the commercial front, the portal provides a platform for putting up announcements for buying or selling cattle. It is also planned to incorporate an e-banking module, it is expected that some banks would come forward to support the direct deposit of the milk payments to the farmers into their accounts and subsequently facilitate withdrawals through smart cards at conveniently located cash dispensing stations. This can be a big boost to the convenience of the dairy farmers.

The portals are created as two tier architecture, with database software hosting and maintaining the data and the server delivering static as well as dynamic the contents. Several technologies are used to create and deliver the contents on the prototype dairy portal.

However, several organizations are working on ICT in dairy cooperative sector. Some have pioneered of e-governance with path breaking solution like MILK-NET with a wide client base in the government department and corporation. Some are working on a range of e-governance solutions with an integrated approach in the long run. The solutions are based on the latest technologies and thus are scalable for the future needs of the dairy cooperative development system.

The MILK-NET, as a Pioneer software of its kind has created software for dairy cooperatives. Software has been integrated and has been implemented to cater to the MIS needs for the first time for any Milk Cooperative Dairy Federation of India in Madhya Pradesh, thus has been named as MILK-NET. It is very economical and easy to use solution with the user oriented approach in the long run.

Conclusion

Knowledge Management (KM) in dairy cooperative sector denotes getting the right knowledge from the right people at right time and helping dairy farmers to share information knowledge and improve the organizational performance of dairy cooperative sector (Primary Milk Producers Societies, District Milk Producers Union, State Level Milk Producers Federations and National Level Milk Producers Federation). The knowledge management programmes can be tied-up with specific dairy organizational objectives, goals, mission, visions to achieve target results, gain contact to competitive advantages, distribute knowledge, know–how, knowledge transfer, etc.

Consequently, KM is extremely very significant in ensuring the growth and development of dairy cooperative sector in India. The current dairy cooperative sector demands for the implementation of the effective and efficient Knowledge Management (KM) strategies and practices. This would depend on the improvement of the KM infrastructure and modernization of dairy cooperative industry in the twenty-first century. It would improve productivity, production, procurement, transportation, processing, and distributions, marketing and sales promotion of milk and milk products. It needs improved use and development of ICT and KM in dairy cooperative industry and would enable better commercial dairy decision making process in the changing business environment. There must be favourable policy development changes and strategies for improving knowledge management in the dairy cooperative sector in the twenty-first century.

REFERENCES

Agricoop.nic.in/stateatglance2003 htm

Binwal, J.C. (2001), Knowledge Management, *IASLIC Bulletin*, 456(2).

Blakie, M.J. and Dent, J.B. (1978), *"Information Systems for Agriculture"*, Applied Science Publishers, Ltd, Ripple Road, Barking, Essex England, UK.

Capart.nic.in

Department of Agriculture, *"Memoirs of the Department of Agriculture, Madras"*, Deptt. of Agriculture, Madras, 1949.

Devika, P. Madalli (2002), Information Resource Management, *DRTC Workshop*. 13-15.

Dharam Narain, *et al.* (1988), *Studies on Indian Agriculture*, OXFORD University Press, Delhi.

Haravu, L.J. (2002), *Lectures on Knowledge Management: Paradigm, Challenges and Opportunities*, Sarada Ranganadan endowment for Library Science.

http://www.brint.com/interview/maeil.htm

in.dir.yahoo.com/Government/Statistics

indiabudget.nic.in

Kim, Seonghee, The Role of Knowledge Professionals for Knowledge Management: *Libraries in the Society. IFLA* Publications, 102-KG. Saur.

Meghnad Desai, *et al.* (1984), *Agrarian Power and Agricultural Productivity in South Asia*, OXFORD University Press.

Patel, N.T. (1982), *Inputs Productivity in Agriculture*, OXFORD and IBH Publishing Co.

Pib.nic.in

Ruddar Datt, Sundaram. K.P.M (2000), *Indian Economy*, S. Chand & Co. Ltd., 459-464pp.

rural.nic.in

Samwel Kakuko Lopoyetum and Selvamani. P., (2006),"Globalisation and Cooperative Movement in India", Third Concept, *International Journal of Ideas*, (20, 237), 15-21.

Samwel Kakuko Lopoyetum and Velu Raj, R. (2005), "Computerisation and Networking (MIS) of Dairy Cooperative Organisations in Tamil Nadu" *Tamil Nadu Journal of Cooperation.*

Samwel Kakuko Lopoyetum, (1999), "Computer Application in the Management Administration of Cooperatives", *Tamil Nadu Journal for Cooperation*, Vol. 91, No. 4.

Samwel Kakuko Lopoyetum, (1999), "Indo-Kenya Dairy Cooperative System; Scope for Dairy Cooperative Development and Replicability Strategy of Indian Model in Kenya", Cooperative Perspective, *Journal of Cooperative Management*. (34, 3).

Samwel Kakuko Lopoyetum, (2003), "Appropriateness of Management Strategies: Are they myth to Cooperatives", *The Cooperator*, (40, 8).

Samwel Kakuko Lopoyetum, (2004), "Challenges and Opportunities before Cooperative Organisations and Appropriate Strategies in the New Millennium" Published in *Problems and Prospects of Cooperative*

Movement: Perspectives For 21st Century by Patil J.F. *et al.* Department of Commerce and Management, Shivaji University, Kolhapur.

Samwel Kakuko Lopoyetum, (2004), "Development and Transformation of Dairy Cooperative Marketing Organisations in the Era of Economic Liberalization and Globalization (WTO)" *Problems and Prospects of Cooperative Movement: Perspectives For 21st Century* by Patil, J.F. *et al.* Department of Commerce and Management, Shivaji University, Kolhapur.

Samwel Kakuko Lopoyetum, (2005),"Global Business Management; Strategies for Cooperative Business Organisation in 21st Century", *Tamil Nadu Journal of Cooperation,* (5, 9), 26-29.

Samwel Kakuko Lopoyetum, (Dec. 2003), "The Dimension of New Generation of Cooperative—21st Century Perspective", *The Tamil Nadu Journal of Cooperative, (11, 2), 11-14.*

Samwel Kakuko Lopoyetum, *et al.* (2003), "Fundamental Management Dimensions of Cooperatives: An Analysis of Major Imperative Issues", *Indian Cooperative Review,* (40, 4), 245.

Samwel Kakuko Lopoyetum, *et al.* "Essential Management Strategies for Cooperative Enterprises and Organisations in the Era of Open Market Economy", *The Cooperator,* (11,3), 88-91.

Sankaran, S. (2005), *Indian Economy,* Marghan Publications.

Singh, Pramod Kumar, (1999-2001), Knowledge Management Application in Libraries and Information Centres-*DRTC Project-2.*

Tiwana, Amrit, (2000), *The Knowledge Management Tool Kit: Practical techniques for building a Knowledge Management System,* Prentice Hall.

www.icar.org.in

www.idrc.ca/pan/telecentre.html

www.indiastat.com

www.linx.Best.com

www.nbu.ac.in

www.ncss.com

www.nemoc.navy.mil

www.search4i.com

www.wikipedia.com

Yates-Mercer, *et al.* (2002), Managing the Paradox: The valuation of Knowledge and Knowledge Management, *Journal of Information Science,* 28(1).

4

Knowledge Management in Research and Development of Indian Agriculture

S.M. Vidya Sekhar, M.S. Prasad, C.R. Thyagaraj* and *S. Ramakrishna*

The global agricultural scenario has been witnessing a sea change for the last two decades. New issues such as global warming and climate change, new pests and diseases, natural resource depletion and degradation, household nutritional security, slowly growing farm profitability, food safety, trade competition, etc., have arisen. The involvement of private sector in agricultural research, education and training is yet another development which need to be harnessed. Thus, agriculture has become more global in its reach, more complex in trade and exchanges, more technologically grounded and ever more challenged with balancing sustainability, productivity, profitability and inclusiveness. In order to address these issues, a paradigm shift is called for in human resource development, research, technology generation, technology dissemination and commercialization. In this endeavour the conventional research approaches need to be supplemented by the cutting-edge technologies requiring multi-disciplinary and multi-institutional inputs. At this juncture "knowledge management" plays a pivotal role.

India is today one of the six fastest growing economies of the world. The business and regulatory environment is evolving and

* Compilation of information from different papers/reports published with due acknowledgement to source information.

moving towards constant improvement. A highly talented, skilled and English-speaking human resource base forms its backbone. To meet the UN Millennium Development Goal of reducing the number of hungry people to half by 2015, there is a need to bridge the huge gap between attainable yield and average yields harvested by the farmers especially in developing countries under fragile environments. India has made impressive strides on the agricultural front during the last three decades. Much of the credit for this success should go to the several million small farming families that form the backbone of Indian agriculture and economy. Policy support, production strategies, public investment in infrastructure, research and extension for crop, livestock and fisheries have significantly helped to increase food production and its availability.

Slow agricultural growth is a concern for policy makers as some two-thirds of India's people depend on rural employment for a living. Current agricultural practices are neither economically nor environmentally sustainable and India's yields for many agricultural commodities are low. Poorly maintained irrigation systems and almost universal lack of good extension services are among the factors responsible. Integrated farming system, agro-processing and renewable energy, are essential both to meet food production targets for increasing food and nutritional security, poverty alleviation and thus livelihood security on sustainable basis. Besides, the ruthless exploitation of natural resources coupled with increasing industrialization is also leading to the energy and rural economy crises. The challenge is, therefore, to assist farmers of developing countries to secure the means to overcome food insecurity and poverty. This calls for new technologies, skills, practices and ways to collaborate. All of this requires that farmers have access to relevant knowledge and information. At the organizational level the knowledge is to be managed so as to disseminate the information to farmers who are the actual end beneficiaries of knowledge.

What is Knowledge Managemen ?

The term "knowledge management" has gained prevalence in recent years due to the revolutionary strides in technology and the rapid evolution of new systems for the gathering, transmission and application of information. A confluence of technologies—television, computers, networking, satellite communications and the internet—constitute the technological basis for the knowledge revolution. Their rapid proliferation over the past decade has made possible movement of information around the world at lightning speed. In this dramatic acceleration in the development of information technologies; in the speed and extent of global knowledge accumulation, dissemination and exchange; in the blurring and transcendence the traditional boundaries need to overcome between fields of knowledge.

- "Knowledge management is the leveraging of collective wisdom to increase responsiveness and innovation", (Thomas M. Koulopoulos).
- "Knowledge management refers to the processes of creating, capturing, transferring and using knowledge to enhance organizational performance," (Public Service Commission of Canada).
- "Knowledge Management (KM) is an integrated, systematic approach for identifying, managing, and sharing all of an enterprise's information assets, including databases, documents, policies and procedures, as well as previously unarticulated expertise and experience resident in individual workers (Joseph Williamson).
- "Knowledge management is the process through which an enterprise uses its collective intelligence to accomplish its strategic objectives" (Ramon Barquin).

Knowledge management caters to the critical issues of organizational adaptation, survival, and competence in the face of increasingly discontinuous environmental change. Essentially, it embodies organizational processes that seek synergestic combination of data and information processing capacity of information technologies, and the creative and innovative capacity of human beings. A guiding and inspiring vision of what India has the opportunity to become by 2020 must take into account the enormous productive potential of knowledge to accelerate the development and transformation of the country. India's rate of economic growth can be substantially increased if the country becomes a superpower in knowledge and if the potentials of information and information technology are fully understood and exploited.

- Knowledge generation and acquisition through scientific discovery, R&D and transfer of technology.
- Knowledge adaptation through innovation to particular fields, needs and operating environments.
- Knowledge dissemination through formal and informal channels from knowledge developers and adapters to those responsible for applying the knowledge in society.
- Knowledge application through skilled action in fields, factories, classrooms, hospitals and every other field of activity to achieve practical results.

Knowledge Gap in Research and Development

The rate of knowledge generation and management in the country is another aspect of the knowledge gap. At the global level, science and technology are expanding at unprecedented rates. There are many ways in which this global knowledge permeates into the domestic economy, but the capacity of any country to adapt and fully harness these advances depends to a significant extent on domestic R&D activity. Knowledge generation in the country is not keeping pace, even proportionately, with the global knowledge revolution.

- India's share of global scientific output in 1998 was only 1.58 per cent of the world's total.
- India's annual output of science papers declined from 13,000 in 1981 to 12,000, while world output has risen from 4 lakh to 7.6 lakhs per year.
- India's share of global scientific citations in 1997 was only 0.7 per cent of the world's total.
- India's rank on the Science Citation Index has fallen from 8 to 13 since the early 1980s.

Knowledge management directly impacts national development when it results in new and improved patentable industrial processes. Every year more than 500,000 new patent applications are filed globally. Of these, China accounts for 96,000 and Korea accounts for 72,000, while India accounts for only 8,000. Korea produces nine times as many patents as India with only twice India's total investment in R&D, suggesting that not only the quantum of investment but the management of R&D activities is a critical determinant of knowledge management.

Crop Productivity Improvement by Knowledge Application [Yield (kg/ha)]

Location	*Crop*	*Local*	*Test*	*Increase*
Tamil Nadu	Tomatoes	31,250	1,05,000	236%
Tamil Nadu	Lint Cotton	335	978	192%
Kerala	Black Pepper	426	1716	303%
Bihar	Maize	1125	2568	128%
Karnataka	Lint Cotton	347	1045	202%

Source : Towards Knowledge Society Vision 2020.

These results illustrate the enormous potential for accelerating India's development by closing the knowledge gap and point to the great importance of improving the quality and relevance of the rural educational system.

Government Initiative towards Knowledge Management in Agricultural Research and Education

Government of India and U.S. Department of Agriculture (USDA) agreed to work together for a new India–US Knowledge Initiative on Agriculture Education, Research, Services and Commercial Linkages, identified the objectives of this Initiative and created the Board of the Knowledge Initiative on Agriculture (AKI) who have, after identifying areas of priority focus, agreed on Work Plan in 2006 which includes :

The initiative aims at attaining excellence in agricultural education, to enhance employability of the graduates, developing human resources to fulfil commitments towards the Millennium Development Goals, and improving quality of life through sustainable rural development including innovative agricultural extension, agri-business programmes and wider participation of women. The AKI is expected to significantly reinvigorate the

US-Indian partnership in agriculture and offer a win-win situation for both the countries and will trigger benefits in perpetuity.

Knowledge Management and Agricultural Policy

The agriculture sector recorded satisfactory growth due to improved technology, irrigation, inputs and pricing policies. Livestock, poultry, fisheries and horticulture are surging ahead in production growth in recent years and will have greater demand in the future. Industrial and service sectors have expanded faster than agriculture sector resulting in declining share of agriculture in national accounts. Despite the structural change, agriculture still remains a key sector, providing both employment and livelihood opportunities to more than 70 per cent of the country's population who live in rural areas. The contribution of small farmers to the national and household food security has been steadily increasing. The water availability for agricultural uses has reached a critical level and deserves urgent attention of all concerned. The agricultural policy for the future (Vision 2020) has to concentrate on managing knowledge based systems at organizational level with respect to :

- Enhancing yield of major commodities.
- Integrated nutrient management.
- Arresting deceleration in total factor productivity.
- Bridging yield gaps.
- Water for sustainable food security.
- Emphasis on rainfed ecosystem.
- Accent on diversification of agriculture and value addition.
- Accent on post-harvest management, value addition and cost-effectiveness.
- Increased investment in agriculture and infrastructures.
- Fighting poverty and hunger.
- Accent on empowering the small farmers.
- Keeping pace with globalisation.
- Exploiting cyber space.

Knowledge and Information is power and will underpin future progress and prosperity. Efforts must be made to strengthen the informatics in agriculture by developing new databases, linking databases with international databases and adding value to information to facilitate knowledge management and decision making at various levels. Development of knowledge based production models for various agro-ecological regimes to forecast the production potential should assume greater importance. Using the remote sensing and GIS technologies, natural and other agricultural resource should be mapped at micro and macro levels and effectively used for land and water use planning as well as agricultural forecasting, market intelligence and e-business, contingency planning and prediction of disease and pest incidences.

REFERENCES

Agriculture Policy: *Vision 2020,* Indian Agricultural Research Institute, New Delhi, Background Papers Vision 2020, submitted to Planning Commission.

Draft US-India Knowledge Initiative on Agriculture–Indian Proposal Department of Agricultural Research and Education Indian Council of Agricultural Research, Krishi Bhavan, New Delhi-110001.

FarmNet: *Farmer Information Network for Agricultural and Rural Development,* Food and Agriculture Organization of the United Nations Research, Extension and Training Division (SDR), World Agricultural Information Centre (WAICENT).

Knowledge and Innovation: *Journal of The KMci,* 1(2), January 15, 2001.

Make a Difference in Sustainable Agriculture Development, New Delhi, India (MAD in SAD) Capacity Enhancement Workshop held on 14th July to 15th July 2007, New Delhi.

Towards a Knowledge Society, *Final Draft for the Vision 2020. Committee* submitted to Planning Commission, New Delhi by Garry Jacobs and N. Asokan, January 1, 2003, The Mothers Service Society, Pondicherry.

5

Knowledge Management : A Backbone for Libraries in Rural Development Programmes

Shobha Kulkarni

Introduction

In the rapidly changing environment, information is the most vital factor in the development and growth of both individuals and organizations. Information becomes knowledge once it is processed in the mind of an individual. In other words, knowledge is information integrated with experience, reflected upon and interpreted in a particular context. Although knowledge can be represented in and often embedded in organizational processes, routines and networks and in document repositories, it is the only cognitive process and intellection of a librarian(s) that can generate knowledge and apply it. Thus, knowledge is the only exploitable and valuable resource, which needs to be managed to create new knowledge for sharing with others. The development in Information and Communication Technology (ICT) put forth a challenge to the libraries to manage this invisible form of information along with the traditional visible information resources. Therefore, unlike those libraries, having collection of publications, the twenty-first century libraries will not only be the store house of information but will be an electronic access points and library managers will be riding the information superhighway, for getting access to the content of the information, i.e., knowledge. In order to improve the services to the users, libraries are applying sound management principles to human resources as a whole who are the carrying vectors of the knowledge.

In this context the article aims to initiate the role of libraries in Rural Development Programmes by applying Knowledge Management initiatives to develop the Knowledge Management System for rural community development.

Knowledge Representation

Peter Drucker in "Post Capitalist Society" has quoted that the basic economic resource—the mean of production—is no longer a capital nor natural resources, nor labour it is and will be knowledge. Knowledge according to Ikujiro Nonanka, has been categorized as Explicit/formal and Tacit/informal. Explicit knowledge can be readily transmitted between individuals formally and systematically whereas tacit knowledge is highly personal and hard to formalize, making it difficult to communicate or share with others.

The current research in knowledge types has categorized another form, i.e., cultural knowledge. It is the filter that helps to place a value on certain parts of knowledge. It is the knowledge that includes the assumption and belief that are used to describe and explain reality as well as the conventions and experience, e.g., a farmer who has a wealth of expertise in water conservation or soil strength as a transferred knowledge from generations cannot articulate as a technical principle. Once the values of scientific principles are attached, it becomes the cultural knowledge. The same forms in the context of libraries may be represented as follows.

The knowledge represented in library environment is the full utilization of information and data coupled with the potential of people's skills, competencies, ideas, intuitions, commitments and motivation as the explicit knowledge. Whereas the tacit knowledge is the knowledge created constantly by people, becomes a powerful commodity and the articulation of personal knowledge with technical principles will form the cultural knowledge.

Knowledge Management

Just as there are numerous definitions of knowledge, there are also numerous definitions of Knowledge Management (KM). To date, no general approach to managing knowledge has been commonly accepted but various diverging notions are noticed while defining KM. However, a simple way of defining KM is that "KM is the process of organizing and sharing the diverse forms of business information created within an organization". In fact, the combination of people, process and technology is essential to orderly articulate, capture, store, access and the share the knowledge for reuse. Therefore, KM is the composite management technique, which establishes relation between information and knowledge. Hence generic model of KM is :

KM = People + Process + Information

Characteristics of KM in Libraries

KM in general relates to unlocking and leveraging the knowledge of individuals so that it becomes available as an organizational resource independent of particular individuals. In libraries KM viewed from an information system perspective and is based on the belief that KM systems can be used to capture and store people's knowledge and make it accessible to others through a searchable application. The characteristics of KM in library follow a new management mode.

1. Human Resource Management is the core of KM in libraries Human beings are the knowledge assets to the organization. Their ability and knowledge level in acquiring and innovating knowledge must be a potential source in developing knowledge resources. The lifelong education and proper training will raise the work efficiency and quality services to the user.
2. Objectives of KM in libraries is to promote knowledge innovation libraries are the important and indispensable link in the research process, i.e., knowledge innovation. They act as bridges for turning results of knowledge innovation into a realistic production forces. Libraries carry out research for construction of digital and virtual

libraries, protection of intellectual property rights in the electronic era, etc.

3. It is a tool for KM in libraries. It will help in knowledge acquisition process. It is possible to link Knowledge sources to knowledge workers through computer networks, i.e., constructing knowledge networks in libraries.
4. KM emphasizes repository view. The gathering, providing and filtering of knowledge as the information which can be further transferred and shared easily through repositories. The expert sharing dimension of KM emphasize the human aspects—cognitive, social, culture, and organizational aspects, in addition to information storage and retrieval.
5. KM enables to enlarge the intellectual properties. KM should enable an organization to effectively store, manage, retrieve and enlarge its intellectual properties.

Knowledge Management Tools

The literature survey shows many technological tools are being used for designing the KM system. Among many, most favourite technological tools used for effective KM system are as follows :

1. *Internet/Extranet*—It allows the seekers to access the information through any browser without any geographical boundary.
2. *Data mining*—It helps to store the structured knowledge.
3. Groupware—It is a popular software used for developing *KM system*—It offers a platform to capture the inter-communication between the people in the organization.

   Lotus notes R5 of IBM, Netscape's Collabra Share, Microsoft exchange, etc., are some of the popular groupware software.
4. *Geographic Information System*—This technology permits the superimposition and manipulation of various kinds of demographic and corporate data on the map.
5. *Technology collaboration*—It helps to activate different communication channels, viz., messaging, discussion group, chat, AV conference for accessing the knowledge.
6. *Web mapping tools*—It helps to manage the online document for KMC.

KM Process in Libraries

Data information and knowledge are the constantly used terms in the resource management process. Knowledge ic created constantly and becomes a powerful commodity of the library. Hence, KM is all about the process of bringing people, information and technology together, which adds value to it to generate and share new knowledge. According to Davenport, KM process is about acquisition, creation, package and application or reuse of knowledge. But in libraries KM process involves following five steps :

1. Knowledge Identification.
2. Knowledge Collection.
3. Knowledge Organization.
4. Knowledge Preservation.
5. Knowledge Dissemination.

1. *Knowledge Identification*: It is essential to any organization to identify the knowledge domains to support the core competencies to get the continuous flow of knowledge about its user's needs and expectation, products and services, finance, employees, etc. It also helps to build the knowledge repositories for future use.

2. *Knowledge Collection*: It is a knowledge generation phase, helps to capture the existing knowledge acquired by the organization as well as that knowledge which is not generated within but collected by some other methods.

3. *Knowledge Organization*: In this stage the tacit or embedded knowledge is codified and stored in knowledge based which can be shared by knowledge mapping tools to those who are in need of it through KM system.

4. *Knowledge Preservation*: The collected and codified knowledge is stored in knowledge base which resides at intranet/ extranet, etc.

5. *Knowledge Dissemination*: The success of effective and efficient utilization of knowledge depends on the way the knowledge dissemination process is designed. It is essential to follow the standard methodology to design knowledge bases and data banks with hypertext links. It also needs efficient query

languages, browsers and navigation systems to retrieve knowledge from knowledge repositories.

The proposed KM processes transformed the image of the library as an important organization in knowledge industry. It also shows that the libraries have a potential to offer innumerable services to any section of the society wherever they are linked/located. The same may be highlighted further by emphasizing the library's participation in rural development programmes through KM initiatives.

Libraries and Rural Development

Rural Development (RD) connotes overall development of rural areas with a view to improve their quality of life of people living there. It is a process through collective efforts aimed at improving the well-being and self-realization of people living in rural areas. The ultimate target of RD is, therefore, the people and not infrastructure. Government and Non-Government Organizations are putting enormous efforts to bridge the so-called "Digital Divide" by initiating so many RD projects. Lots of money has been spent to promote different programmes and schemes to uplift the standard of rural mass, especially in literacy, education, health care, population, environment, etc. But one has to admit that even after putting so many efforts the reality is far off.

Library as a Nodal Agency

The RD programmes are never planned by giving due consideration to overall problems of rural mass or by assessing proper needs of the rural community. Here the libraries can play an important role in assessing and studying the actual needs of the rural mass. It may use knowledge repositories by integrating various parameters of RD and maintain proper balance between rural society and technology. It acts as an intermediary between various government initiated RD projects and knowledge sources collected from rural mass or from various agro based products. A close search of physical as well as Internet could hardly yield any mention about libraries role in RD. Public libraries in certain States are fulfilling this role to some extent but not as a mission. Libraries, therefore, can become a Community Information Centre by utilizing KM initiatives to give the need based information to rural mass and thereby act as an important nodal agency for RD.

Parameters of RD

The needs of rural mass in terms of information can be assessed by studying various parameters of RD. As it is intended to improve the social and economic condition, it must be designed clearly so that the specific need will be fulfilled and achieve more productivity. Increase in productivity can be achieved by both direct and indirect methods.

Direct methods include providing good quality of seeds and fertilizers to farmers at subsidized rates, helping them to use traditional tacit knowledge about soil conditions, weather forecasting in farming, using their cultural knowledge in developing/modifying harvesting machinery, etc., promoting village arts and crafts, providing proper access to information about market to rural products and services. Examples of these applications are–Warananagar Milk Cooperative, RASI project of Tamil Nadu, Kittur experiment of Karnataka, Dnyan Kendras project of Ms Swaminathan Research Foundation, white revolution movement of Verghese Kurien for empowering women, Gyandoot of MP, PURA vision of Ex-President, APJ Abdul Kalam, etc. Whereas the indirect methods cover promoting literacy, education, family planning, health care, economic well-being, socio-cultural conditions, etc.

Rural development is a continuous process and always there is a possibility of developing new knowledge for further development. Libraries, therefore, can articulate all such RD parameters in knowledge depository for future use.

Knowledge Management Systems

The reference desk of library can be treated as Community Information Centre to satisfy the local users' demands. In the library, knowledge is captured in various forms and developed as comprehensive collection of physical as well as electronic or digital information. Explicit knowledge in the form of various government schemes and projects for RD may either be hyper linked if available in e-form or the necessary data may be captured and identified. Similarly the knowledge about various methods used for easy marketing of agro products also captured. In addition to this, the expertise skills represented as tacit knowledge need to be recorded either by way of continuous observation or by developing a dialogue. The knowledge thus captured is organized for storage and retrieval purpose by using Knowledge Mapping Tools. Such an organized knowledge further stored in Knowledge Repository and then retrieved through Knowledge Management System (KMS).

KMS is an online computerized system containing the expertise, knowledge, sources, procedures, policies, work-flows products, and services, etc., about the particular knowledge domain. It is essentially used to coordinate process and contents for performing any knowledge specific task in the library.

The knowledge repository for rural development may thus include knowledge on various government schemes and projects, policies and procedure, sources of markets for agro-products and embedded skills and practices followed while cultivation/farming. The efficient query languages like PostGre SQL for searching or groupware systems like Microsoft exchange, Lotus notes R 5, etc., as a navigation tool or rule-based systems are used to retrieve the knowledge from knowledge repository. The knowledge management system for RD is thus a collaboration of knowledge repository, software for knowledge retrieval, intranet/extranet for accessing knowledge and different services to rural community. Accordingly the needs of the rural community can be fulfilled by matching the knowledge resources captured in knowledge repository in KMS and the disseminated knowledge may further be communicated by using intranet. The retrieved knowledge may also be shared for solving problems among rural community, making decisions about application to any specific scheme, and developing new ideas in farming or learning new technique. Knowledge thus used and applied may indicate the level of fulfilment in various Rural Development Programmes. The KMS thus available at library's reference desk enables to achieve the well-being of rural community and thereby create a new piece of knowledge in the form of users' feedback and analysis.

Conclusion

According to Skyme, a good KM is achieved by enriching the existing knowledge base, knowledge repositories and data warehouses. Therefore, KM is an art of creating value for organization's tangible/formal and intangible/informal assets. It is like a backbone to library manager who may be recognized as knowledge manager to set KM as a strategic priority to obtain users' satisfaction. KM techniques thus entails extracting relevant knowledge from multiple sources along with their context and being able to collate them meaningfully for developing the fruitful relationship between human beings and the captured knowledge. As KM is successful in narrow domain and RD being one of the highly referred domain by government organizations, it is then the right area for application of KM. Libraries can use KM initiatives as a potential backbone in RD programmes.

REFERENCES

Banka Bihari Chand. Knowledge Management: Tools and Techniques for Librarians, 2001, *JLIS*, 26(2), 175-186.

Binwal, J.C. Knowledge Management, *IASLIC Bull.*, 2001, 46(2), 65-78.

Broadbent, Marianne. Phenomena of Knowledge Management: What Does it Mean to the Information Professional? *Information Outlook, 1998*, 2(5), 1998, 23-36.

Davenport, Thomas H. Some Principles of Knowledge Management <http://www.bus.utexas.edu>

Mukhopadhyaya, Anand Deb. Integrated Rural Development (IRD) and Information Support System (ISS), *IASLIC Bull, 2003*, 48(3), 131-140.

Mutalik, V.J. Symbiosis of libraries and rural development, *Herald of Library Science*, 2005, 44(1-2), 64-71.

Savanur, S.K. In search of measurable issues in rural development, In National seminar on role of public libraries in rural development, July 2002.

Vedakumari, V. Information and Communication Technologies (TCT) for rural development, *Journal of Rural Development*, 2005, 24(3), 399-408.

6
Transforming Lives with Village Resource Centres (VRCs)

Jayaprakash, R.

Introduction

Technological divide is an important factor in widening the rich-poor divide both among and within nations since the onset of the industrial revolution in Europe. With explosive progress in many areas of technology, like information, space, bio and nano-technology, this divide is increasing. The challenge now is to enlist technology as an ally in the movement for economic, social and gender equity.

AVS in partnership with MSSRF Chennai and ISRO started a Village Resource Centre at Kottakkal. It is mainly aimed to establish a content generating station related to herbal cultivation and ayurvedic knowledge.

How it Works ?

The VRC is working in a multilevel concept. Village Knowledge Centres (VKC), networking throughout the area is owned by the community people are in the root level. They generate community driven knowledge, make request and pass to Village Resource Centres (VRC). VRC will collect the requests and information from various VKCs. They will form a data bank and will pass to the Data providers like MSSRF/ISRO where the expert team will analyze and process the data. After that, the information will pass to the root level through same channel.

The whole system worked on the "intranet" run by ISRO. The required bandwidth and satellite connection is provided by them free of cost. We are working as a data analyzing expert body in Ayurvedic field and as a query generating end in case of other areas like agriculture, fisheries, etc. The VKCs will gather all the queries from grass root level and will pass to VRC.

Content Generation and Capacity Building in AVS VRC

A community database collection was the first attempt in the field. The area contains different communities like fishermen, farmers, tribals, etc. So the database has to address various problems from different communities. Apart from that we have a strong database of Ayurvedic field cultivation and practice. We have an expert body to analyse and process data in ayurveda coming from other VKCs and to reply their queries.

Queries about whether from fisherman and about various cultivation methods from farmers has to be processed. Significant is the information on wave heights that provides a 12-hour prediction for wave heights in the Arabian sea. The images are downloaded from U.S. Navy website and the same is delivered to the VKC in harbour area. By introducing buy-back system, we promoted herbal cultivation among farmers. Also facilitates e-trading for their products. Apart from this we also started computer education for tenth class students with the help of "Microsoft unlimited potential programmes".

Tele-medicine—A New Light to Poor

Heart related health problems can be well addressed in our VRC. We have facility to take ECG and to send it to a multi speciality hospital in Chennai. The cardiac expert will examine the ECG and a live consultation will be scheduled. The patient can lively interact with the doctor through video conferencing. By this the poor village people can access the hi-end treatment facilities at free of cost.

Challenges Faced

Field work among illiterate fishermen and old farmers were really a difficult task. The scientific cultivation methods are always mixed with their traditional knowledge. The herbal cultivation has to be inspected on field from time to time in order to ensure the purity of the cultivating herbs. This needs a lot of field staff but cannot be afforded by the VKC due to the financial constraints. In buy-back system, the product value was highly fluctuating and made the farmers difficult to cultivate. Apart from the cardiac patients, other streams are also coming forward for treatment which we could not handle at present. The fund for running all this has to be found to some extent from its activities. So we have to plan some fund generating activities for VRC.

Tackling the Problems

A literacy mission is successfully implemented in rural areas to ensure the smooth communication. Rigorous training sessions are planned for the farmers to make them aware of scientific methods of cultivation. The class room sessions are also conducted to solve their queries through video conferencing with experts. Volunteer field staff is trained from farmer groups. After a proper field survey about the diseases of this area, we are supposed to request the service of more medical expert through tele-medicine. Despite dealing with problems putting sincere efforts, the project could not sustain 2009 onwards.

7

Knowledge Management for Rural Development : Practical Aspects

Tilak Raj Kapoor

Introduction

Knowledge Management is buzzword that is often mistaken. The basic question is—can we really manage knowledge. A quick answer would be "Yes"; but that is debatable for various reasons including information and knowledge behaviour of individuals. Knowledge cannot be managed—information leading to knowledge can be accumulated, made accessible and acquired but what we are managing, in fact, is just the processes that lead to the scope of availability of knowledge when one needs it. The processes involved are related to creating, disseminating, sharing and most importantly using knowledge. While designing management framework for these processes one has to bear in mind various questions that play role in these processes.

For simplicity of understanding, as it prevails, there is no harm in assuming that Knowledge Management can be termed as it is but in fact it is management of processes involved in creating, disseminating, sharing and most importantly using knowledge.

When it comes to managing processes, the first obvious question is what the processes are? Knowledge Management cannot be defined in a universally applicable framework so is the case of processes involved in it. However, there are some general principles that play a guiding role in defining Knowledge Management framework.

The common Pyramid shaped Data-Information-Knowledge-Wisdom model gives an impression that the Knowledge Management initiatives are founded on huge data. That is not the case. Depending on the needs defined by the end-product, the Knowledge Management initiatives will find its own structure. The knowledge needs of rural sector can be broadly divided into two categories; one is needed by the rural development planners and the other is needed by rural societies/communities especially for performance improvement. Rural opportunity matrix is complex for both the planners and also the rural societies. Effective utilization of rural resources is not a simple question to answer in absence of appropriate knowledge. To assess appropriateness of knowledge there are some basic issues that are discussed in this chapter.

Forms of Knowledge

1. *Theoretical Knowledge*

Theoretical knowledge is grounded in both what people know and how they know it. This is termed "theoretical" knowledge because of its basis in the use of logic and reason in an attempt to create generally applicable theory. Theoretical knowledge can most easily be illustrated with examples from the natural sciences. Whilst ancient humans no doubt had "know-how" they had no systematic manner of ordering or understanding this "know-how".

This is not to degrade the value of "know-how" or specific "skills", indeed there are ample evidence of skill, where the theoretical knowledge comes into play is when this skill is considered and reflected upon, enabling the individual to generalize knowledge from their specific information. This is not to say that their generalizations are necessary correct or true, rather that there is a recognition of logic in the thought process. Likewise it would be wrong to dismiss skills; know-how is a carrier of complex forms of knowledge, often unacknowledged, which is why skills are tacit knowledge, which is to say that it is unspoken or silent. Thus, the knowledge exists, it is simply not explicit, yet this does not discount its value. Theoretical knowledge does not exclude indigenous theoretical knowledge, which is local knowledge founded on scientific and deductive enquiry.

Both local and universal methods of knowledge testing and sharing are valid forms of knowledge mediation. The important point is that knowledge "can be challenged, tested, repeated, transmitted over time and verified by others", if this is not the case then it is faith or instinct, not theoretical knowledge. Thus, theoretical knowledge seeks to explain phenomena using reasoning in an attempt to create theories which can explain why certain events occur.

2. *Declarative Knowledge*

Declarative knowledge is the ability to name or describe a certain phenomena or concept; it "refers to concepts without making inferences about them, and is factual in nature". This distinction is important as we must distinguish between tacit (silent, unspoken) knowledge and declarative (codified) knowledge.

Whilst declarative knowledge is a part of process knowledge, it is restricted to dealing with the naming and describing of phenomena, it is by its nature factual.

Because of the relative "simplicity' of declarative knowledge it is often easier to access and record this form of knowledge. Declarative knowledge is relatively explicit, people tend to be aware of their ability to name or describe a particular object or phenomena. The descriptive knowledge is much easier to access and record than tacit knowledge, which is a more difficult form of knowledge to document.

3. *Procedural Knowledge*

In contrast to declarative knowledge, process knowledge is that which is required to intervene or take action. "Procedural knowledge refers to knowledge that is needed to execute procedures which enable experts to implement their tacit knowledge to solve problems". This can take the form of a specific skill (or skills) about how to do something as well as mental knowledge about what to do. Much procedural knowledge exists in a tacit form; people are usually unaware that they are using process knowledge which is what distinguishes their knowledge as tacit when they seek to solve problems. This can take the form of automatic behaviours, such as recognizing that the weather is cold (declarative knowledge) and deciding to wear a coat in order to stay warm (process knowledge). Here a person may not be conscious that they are using knowledge (whereas they may be aware of their knowledge of the weather and temperature scales) yet they are in fact taking in many inputs of tacit knowledge, ordering them and making a decision. The same is true with more complex decisions, where an expert may not be conscious of using process knowledge "while its existence is proven by the problem-solving capabilities of the expert".

Yet because these problem solving mechanisms are based upon both tacit knowledge, past experience, reflection, theoretical knowledge and perhaps beliefs, process knowledge is necessarily bound to a certain domain.

It is in the application of this tacit knowledge that the use of procedural knowledge is particularly interesting. Despite the tacit nature of the knowledge it is vital that we incorporate process knowledge into our understanding of what constitutes knowledge. How process knowledge mobilizes many forms of tacit knowledge and combines them with prior experience, theoretical understanding and, perhaps also, dynamic knowledge.

4. *Dynamic Knowledge*

Dynamic knowledge is the knowledge of innovation; it draws on the three previous forms of knowledge, and produces new ideas and concepts. From a research perspective dynamic knowledge is the creation of new knowledge (or the application of existing knowledge to novel environments). Whilst it includes a collection of theoretical, tacit and procedural knowledge, the distinguishing factor is that there is new knowledge being created. The creation of new knowledge is not constrained to only the scientific community; indeed a strong argument can be made for the strength of indigenous knowledge creation. The other key aspect of dynamic knowledge is that it is open to change and reflection. The search for new knowledge is tireless, as the creation of new understanding creates new areas of the unknown, a phenomenon described as "the growth of ignorance". Thus, new knowledge produces more questions and avenues for enquiry, making dynamic knowledge an unceasing process. Yet this growth of ignorance can be not only relative but can include knowledge destruction.

The distinguishing feature of dynamic knowledge is that it seeks new information and attempts to apply it in creative ways. The interesting point to note is that this cycle of experimentation, rejection, adaptation and use is very similar to the research process. Yet the dynamics of knowledge is not only a one way process as it is often discussed in the literature. The knowledge loss is a defining characteristic of the "dynamics" of the knowledge system.

5. *Not Just Information*

Knowledge is much more than just information. Data, information and facts may exist but it is only when human activity is applied that this information becomes knowledge. So, an academic journal article contains all sorts of information and data, much of which refers to knowledge such as theory or results from an experiment. However, the scientific article only contributes to knowledge when it is read and interpreted by human activity.

The human factor is the crucial distinction between information and knowing. This distinction is important as it marks the ability to understand information, to interpret this information in terms of local conditions and to then act upon this information. Thus, computers are information stores and not knowledge devices, whilst computers can amass and compute immense amount of information, there still requires a human input to make sense of this data. Pieces of paper and bytes, by themselves, know nothing; they are nothing more than representations of the human communication of knowledge. Even if this data is transferred to a human, they only become "informed" about the subject if they understand it. Because of this human factor it becomes very difficult to quantify knowledge. Whilst we can measure information by using word counts, megabytes and gigabytes, pages and the like, we cannot so easily gauge knowledge. In the case of declarative knowledge it may be possible to gather everything that a person knows on a given subject and quantify this. However, the procedural knowledge involved in using this declarative knowledge is much more difficult to appraise. Thus, we seek to understand not so much "what" is known but rather "how" it is known. Thus, the knowledge process is a question of how people create, interpret, apply and share information. The actual subject of the information is less important than the manner in which it is communicated and interpreted, the point at which it becomes knowledge.

Knowledge Management and Knowledge Maps

Most knowledge mapping efforts are directed towards mapping documents and other sources by using the domain content of these documents. While these maps can be useful for people engaged in the actual use of the knowledge, this does not necessarily hold for people concerned about managing the knowledge. There may be questions on properties like :

- How stable the knowledge is?
- Whether the proficiency level of the knowledge is adequate?
- How accessible this knowledge is and other aspects?

These properties of knowledge cannot be answered unless we have knowledge about knowledge. If this meta-knowledge is not defined with the document we are left with a pile of documents to look for. In absence of meta-knowledge knowledge mapping efforts fail to provide the information needed to deal with many knowledge management issues.

Knowledge requirements would depend on the tasks being performed. If these tasks are not known in advance appropriate knowledge mapping would be absent in Knowledge Management.

An advance knowledge of targeted business processes and tasks leads to a framework that can be used to design and build a knowledge mapping environment that can support knowledge management for possible knowledge questions.

Each organization, even with skilled knowledge workers, needs to invest efforts in Knowledge Management to be able to continuously improve outcome. The objective of knowledge management is to bring in smartness to actions of the society. A smart organization or society knows in advance the knowledge map encompassing its working domain, has persons that have this knowledge, and uses technologies in a smart way to support its knowledge workers. Obviously it also has a well defined framework and system to acquire and disseminate knowledge.

Who would Manage Knowledge?

Knowledge Management in fact being process management has to be done by the organization itself. In the process of Knowledge Management, organizations come across various questions. Examples of those questions and solutions are:

- How to enhance the innovative power of the organization?
- How to ensure that the knowledge and vision of organizational people becomes knowledge of the organization?

What technical support and organizational incentives are required to stimulate the exchange of knowledge, experience and vision, and the application of new ideas?

Is everyone doing well with knowledge management?

- How to monitor efficacy of knowledge management?
- What people think about knowledge does the organization have?
- How to measure smartness of people in the organization?
- What communication and documentation exists in the organization and how knowledge can be extracted from it and how it will be stored and communicated?

Do we have similar organization beyond our own organizational boundaries? Can these organizations be involved to create global resources and common pool of knowledge created from the knowledge of individual organization?

How the Technology and Science can be made to Play its Role in Leveraging KM?

There is a clear distinction between *using* the knowledge and *managing* the knowledge. Similarly, there is a clear distinction between knowledge contribution and knowledge creation. There are different tasks that require mapping of different aspects of knowledge. Anyone can contribute knowledge but creating accessible, understandable and applicable knowledge objects is a skilled domain in a formal scenario.

There can be various models that can be defined on the basis of a set of criteria consisting of cyclical nature, knowledge specificity, separating management from work, appropriate grain size, tool independency and time horizon.

Available knowledge management literature suggests a set of agreed upon properties that could be used in constructing knowledge management relevant knowledge maps.

Characteristics for describing the demand :

- time related : the knowledge is needed at a certain time
- type : demand for a product/service, result, person..
- level : oriented on individual, group or organization quality quantity rigidity (what possibilities are there to redefine the demand)

Knowledge Management Macro Level Processes

Acquisition: It is the process of identifying knowledge in the environment and transforming it into a representation that can be internalized and/or used. It has following sub-tasks :

- The first sub-task is identifying the knowledge that includes locating, accessing, valuing, and/or filtering knowledge from outside sources.
- The second sub-task is capturing that includes extracting, collecting, and/or gathering knowledge deemed to be sufficiently valid and useful. Obviously, it includes validating the identified knowledge.
- The third sub-task is organizing captured knowledge that includes distilling, refining, orienting, interpreting, packaging, assembling, and/or transforming captured knowledge into representations that can be understood and processed by another knowledge management manipulation activity.
- The fourth sub-task is transferring organized knowledge that includes communication channel identification and selection, scheduling and sending.

Selection: It is the process of identifying needed knowledge within an organization's existing knowledge resources and providing it in an appropriate representation to an activity that needs it. It has basically the same sub-tasks as under "acquiring knowledge", but the domain is within the organization.

Internalization: It is the process of incorporating or making the knowledge a part of the organization. It has the following sub-tasks:

- The first sub-task is assessing and valuing that includes determining the suitability of the knowledge.
- The second sub-task is targeting that includes identifying knowledge resources that are to be impacted by the knowledge produced by internalization.
- The third sub-task is structuring that includes representing knowledge to be conveyed in the appropriate form for the targets.
- The fourth sub-task is delivering that includes modifying existing knowledge resources, depositing, storing, updating, disseminating, distributing and sharing knowledge, it also involves channel identification and choice, scheduling, and sending.

Use: Use of knowledge comprises of *generating knowledge* and *externalizing knowledge.* These are described below:

Generating: It is the process of producing knowledge by processing existing knowledge. It has the following sub-tasks:

- The first sub-task is monitoring the organization's knowledge resources and the external environment by invoking selection and/or acquisition activities as needed.
- The second sub-task is evaluating selected or acquired knowledge in terms of its utility and validity.
- The third sub-task is producing knowledge from a previously existing base, this may involve creating, synthesizing, analyzing, and constructing knowledge.
- The fourth sub-task is transferring the produced knowledge for externalization and/or internalization, includes channel identification and choice, scheduling and sending.

Externalizing: It is the process of using existing knowledge to produce external outputs for release into the environment. It has the following sub-tasks :

- The first sub-task is targeting the output that includes determining what needs to be produced.
- The second sub-task is producing that includes applying, embodying, controlling and leveraging existing knowledge to produce output.
- The third sub-task is transferring that includes packaging and delivering the projections that have been produced for the targets, this includes channel identification and choice, scheduling and sending.

Categories of Questions involved in Knowledge Management

There are five basic types of questions: (i) Factual; (ii) Convergent; (iii) Divergent; (iv) Evaluative; and (v) Combination.

Socrates believed that knowledge and awareness were an intrinsic part of each learner. Thus, in exercising the craft of good teaching an educator must reach into the learner's hidden levels of knowing and awareness in order to help the learner reach new levels of thinking.

Through the art of thoughtful questioning one can extract not only factual information, but aid learners in: connecting concepts, making inferences, increasing awareness, encouraging creative and imaginative thought, aiding critical thinking processes, and generally helping learners explore deeper levels of knowing, thinking, and understanding.

1. *Factual*—Soliciting reasonably simple, straightforward answers based on obvious facts or awareness. These are usually at the lowest level of cognitive or affective processes and answers are frequently either right or wrong.
2. *Convergent*—Answers to these types of questions are usually within a very finite range of acceptable accuracy. These may be at several different levels of cognition—comprehension, application, analysis, or ones where the answerer makes inferences or conjectures based on personal awareness, or on material read, presented or known.
3. *Divergent*—These questions allow learner to explore different avenues and create many different variations and

alternative answers or scenarios. Correctness may be based on logical projections, may be contextual, or arrived at through basic knowledge, conjecture, inference, projection, creation, intuition, or imagination. These types of questions often require knowledge contributors/learners to analyze, synthesize, or evaluate a knowledge based and then project or predict different outcomes.

Answering divergent questions may be aided by higher levels of affective functions. Answers to these types of questions generally fall into a wide range of acceptability. Often correctness is determined subjectively based on the possibility or probability. Frequently, the intention of these types of divergent questions is to stimulate imaginative and creative thought, or investigate cause and effect relationships, or provoke deeper thought or extensive investigations. And, one needs to be prepared for the fact that there may not be right or definitely correct answers to these questions.

Divergent questions may also serve as larger contexts for directing inquiries, and as such may become what are known as "essential" questions that frame the content of an entire course.

4. *Evaluative*—These types of questions usually require sophisticated levels of cognitive and/or emotional judgment. In attempting to answer evaluative questions, knowledge contributors/learners may be combining multiple logical and/or affective thinking process, or comparative frameworks. Often an answer is analyzed at multiple levels and from different perspectives before the answerer arrives at newly synthesized information or conclusions.
5. *Combinations*—These are questions that blend any combination of the above.

Provocative questions are ones that entice and cannot be answered with easy answers. These questions can be used to motivate and frame content or are essential questions. In the initial categorization above they would be either complex divergent questions or more sophisticated combination questions like divergent/evaluative ones.

Knowledge Management Activities

Knowledge Management consists of four management activities:

- *Coordination* : This involves the determination of what knowledge activities to perform in what sequence, which participants will perform them, and what knowledge resources will be operated on by each.
- *Control* : Ensuring that the needed knowledge resources and processes are available in sufficient quality and quantity.
- *Measurement* : The valuation of knowledge resources and processors.
- *Leadership* : Establishing enabling conditions for fruitful knowledge management.

These four activities are supported by a set of factors to be considered, phrased as questions.

Conclusion

Knowledge Management initiatives must be supported by appropriate understanding of domain in context of its knowledge needs. This has to be done through exhaustive "System Requirement Study" in knowledge context related to business domain. It is necessary to identify various role players and understand their role in Knowledge Management. In identifying roles it is necessary to relate skill level to the roles. In order to ensure that the knowledge is available when it is needed it is necessary to structure accessibility in a way that is intuitive. It is also necessary to understand that the knowledge needs within the society or organization can be different depending on the role in the business domain. Though it would be necessary to answer what is? How to? shall have priority over it, else it would be simply information management and not the knowledge management. There must be a strong communication network that keeps on interviewing knowledge users on the issues of effectiveness of outcome of Knowledge Management.

8

A Framework for Knowledge Management Practices in Rural Development : The Indian Context

Neelam Prasad

Introduction

The age old concept of development was labour, land and capital to which has now been added knowledge. To develop knowledge, information is required and be properly managed. Knowledge Management (KM) is a relatively new concept of management. It has been accelerated by the rapid developments of Information Communication and Technology (ICT). Facilities assøciated with ICT are many. It expedites the exchange of data, information and documents. In another group it facilitates communication, content management systems to organize and retrieve documents, expert system, data and text mining systems, etc. Various methods of communication, e.g., e-mail, fax, phone and video-conferences have now become routine.

At the pace at which technology is advancing it will revolutionize the way we communicate and interact with each other. Exchange of data and information will become faster and easier, but users will have to face the challenge of selecting relevant data, information and documents. It is, therefore, important to understand the potentials and limitations and also to recognize the difference between data, information and knowledge.

Table 8.1: Data Information and Knowledge

Level	*Type*	*Description*
simple ↑	Data	Data consists of numbers, e.g., prices, quantities, records on income, temperature and so on. Data is not meaningful in itself but raw material for creating a message (information).
	Information	Any information contains a message and pursues an objective. The problem with information is that the sender of it must check if the receiver understands it as was intended by the sender. Therefore, information materials must always be treated before mass reproduction begins.
	Explicit Knowledge	Explicit knowledge can be described, written down and documented (i.e., encoded). Behavioural rules, agricultural calendars, curative treatments, scientific theories represent explicit knowledge. Explicit knowledge is largely acquired in formal educational settings.
↓ complex	Implicit Knowledge	Implicit knowledge is acquired through enculturation and experiences in one's socio-cultural environment. Implicit knowledge is complex, logical and value laden but often unconsciously acquired and learned. Therefore, it is difficult to explain to an outsider who does not belong to the same social group. Due to its implicit characteristics it also is difficult to document. Much of our daily routines, behaviour, ideas about good life, success, tasty foods rest on implicit knowledge.

Sources: Michael Polanyi, 1966; Nonaka/Takeuchi, 1995, Davenport/Prusak 1998.

It is good to know the distinction between data, information, explicit and implicit knowledge. Knowledge of distinction helps to understand that ICT is most useful for shuffling data and information and to some extent in transferring documented knowledge. ICT is of little use when it comes to transfer complex or implicit knowledge. Knowledge managers face the challenge of not only in organizing encoded knowledge resources but also in bringing knowledgeable people together, so that they can share their distinct knowledge and experiences. By providing a creative and relaxed atmosphere people can synergize their insight and also update themselves with new and interesting things. Innovations germinate from creative or combination of explicit and implicit knowledge, in addition to developments of ICT.

Principles for Knowledge Sharing

To create innovative knowledge a few principles have to be observed. Leaders and/or managers have to translate these principles to action, especially by setting examples to their subordinates. The principles may be enumerated as follows :

- By building good relationship on personal acquaintance and trust.
- By creating a shared knowledge based by way of vocational training, joint discussion, publication, team building and job rotation.
- By providing places and time for exchange of ideas.
- By giving incentive to those who share their knowledge.
- By providing opportunities to employees so they become more creative.
- By appreciating ideas, irrespective of their status.
- By encouraging employees to bring forward the knowledge gaps and project failures.

Knowledge Services for Rural Areas

Knowledge is key to economic, social and political development. Rural areas do not only require knowledge for agricultural production. They also need to know about markets, prices, standards, alternative sources of income, organization, and political reforms. Rural areas are structurally disadvantaged in accessing knowledge. To empower them, they must be provided with knowledge efficiently, through the following methods :

- Extension.
- Qualification.
- Research.
- Information and communication technologies.

Policy of Indian Government

The vision of Ministry of Information Technology is to provide services through ICT to improve the economic status of all sections of the society in a new and unique way. The vision addresses age-old problems in the fields of :

- Education,
- Health,
- Rural development,
- Alleviation of poverty,
- Employment,
- Agriculture, etc.

Apart from improving the above-mentioned services ICT may facilitate information transparency, good governance, empowerment, participative management and grass roots democracy.

Some Community Projects of Rural India

Akashganga 'the milky way'—For rural dairy producers (co-operative venture), this venture was started in Anand, Gujarat for rural milk producers. ICT facilitates rural milk producers in timely collection of milk and also of payments thus generates higher profits for them. Earlier all activities of milk collection was done manually at District Cooperative Societies (DCS). In the manual process milk often got spoilt due to climatic conditions and producers had to wait in long queues to receive payments. Transactions in basic milk collection comprise the following steps :

- Use of electronic weighing scale to weigh milk,
- Use of Milko Tester for fat testing,
- Generation/capture of unique member ID by PC software, and
- Printing of a pay slip with all data and amount due.

Apart from milk collection data Dairy Information Services Kiosk offers several animal husbandry related services. Akashganga is used 365 days a year for more than six hours at 400 locations.

Benefits of Akashganga are :

- Speedier milk collection;
- Shorter queues in payment distribution;

- Lower prevalence of corrupt practices due to maintenance of DCS accounts.

Information Village Experiment—Empowering rural people through access to timely and relevant information, the project is based in Pondicherry. The project is a clear example of how ICT can change the life of poor marginal farmers. A local area network of over ten villages has been set up with a hub or Value Addition Centre (VAC). The VAC comprises of two Internet dial-up access modes which collects and further transmits relevant information to the village network. The villages are the "information shops" or Village Knowledge Centre (VKC). These villages are connected by a hybrid wire and wireless network consisting of PCs with multimedia tools, printers, scanners, telephones, modems, VHF duplex radio devices and e-mail connectivity for data and voice transfer.

This experiment has been successful due to involvement of villagers from its early stages. The VAC has generated and made available on the network many databases which are community need based and in the native language (Tamil) using I-LEAP. The villagers have been empowered by having access to information on health, credit, input price and availability, transportation, pest surveillance, agronomic practices, weather, etc. Women workers too have benefited by negotiating better wages for themselves from the information available through VAC.

Wired Villages of Warna—It's role in village development, government aided project. This project is for a relatively well off rural area. A state-of-the-art computer communication network is to be established in twenty five cooperative enterprises. The objective is to :

- To make available information on agriculture, medical, and education through Internet;
- To create a database of the villages based on various criteria;
- To provide tele-education at different levels, primary and higher education;
- To establish Geographical Information System (GIS) for improved administration and land records in the seventy villages surrounding Warna.

This IT-based project will benefit villages in viewing and printing their land records, milk collection activities, sugarcane cultivation and movement, etc. This may make administration approachable and transparent.

Gyandoot "Messenger of Information"—Its role in social engineering, government aided project. It is an intranet in Dhar district of Madhya Pradesh connecting rural cyber cafés catering to the everyday needs of the masses. A unique government-to-citizen (G2C) e-commerce activity aimed at creating a cost effective, replicable, economically self-reliant model to bring the benefits of IT in the rural population. Its success is due to its target of people's information interest such as rates of agriculture production, land record rights, computer training, caste certificates, online redressal of public grievances, health services, e-mail, rural matrimonial alliances, online employment exchange, local weather, application form for jobs, etc.

TARAhaat "Star Market Place"—Connecting rural India to the global village, an NGO initiative (Development Alternatives). This project is for North India aimed at sustainable development in the rural areas. It is an Internet based service with connectivity in the villages through cyber centres known as TARAkendras. Information from these centres can be had in the language of choice, English, Hindi, and Punjabi. Information provided is on all aspects, e.g., social services, health, market, entertainment, etc. It also connects urban and oversea consumers to rural craftspeople. Income generated through the services of TARAhaat is not only for rural people but also for its self-sustenance.

E-Chaupals—Assistance to marginal village farmers with IT base, a corporate house enterprise, ICT. It covers nine States and 36,500 villages and has empowered farmers. The project has started with improved productivity of land and quality of crops by informing and educating the farmers about farming methods, weather prediction, etc. With improved production marketing of agricultural produce are cost effective, therefore, price received have improved. All this have uplifted the life of the people associated with the project.

Similar ICT based Projects have been initiated in Pakistan for Rural Development.

For sustainable rural development it is essential that experts, researchers and farmers come together to exchange and understand knowledge held by each other. ICT is only a media for accelerating the knowledge, but to build a base it is necessary to:

- build mutual trust and respect;
- develop a common language;
- create a shared knowledge basis;
- welcome and appreciate other's knowledge;
- show a learning attitude;
- spend time together for exchange of ideas; and
- spend time together working and investigating.

With better knowledge management practices sustainability of development increases, therefore, it is necessary that we adopt and plan knowledge with care before embarking on any project.

REFERENCES

Gyandoot (2000), Gyandoot the purveyor of knowledge, available at: *www.gyandoot.nic.in*

Hess, C.G. (2006), Knowledge Management and Knowledge Systems for Rural Development, *READER: GTZ Knowledge Management*, 1-9.

Mahmood, Khalid (2006), Multipurpose community tele-centres for rural development in Pakistan, *The Electronic Library*, 23(2), 204-230.

Rao, Siriginidi Subba (2004), Role of ICTs in India's rural community information systems, *Info*, 6(4), 261-269.

TARAhaat (2000), TARAhaat, available at: *www.digitaldividend.org*

9

ICT Enabled Knowledge Management in Agriculture

V. Suresh Babu and *M. Padmaja Sudhir*

Introduction

Development is an exercise towards betterment in quality of life. Sometimes access to information is action towards development. All activities related to the development aims at building the nation and socio-economic transformation. The more the development of villages the more progress of the country. Information if communicated with the help of technology to reach people in remote areas is possible only with the help of ICT. Development is now in the hands of people using technological communication and information for rural people requirements. These exercises are very well put in practice by some of the non-governmental organizations to give support and strengthen the implementing capacity of the rural based activities. The generation gap in development of ICT tools categorize them into "old" and "new" wherein radio, television and telephone are labelled old and the computers, mobiles, 3D cameras, wireless technology, Internet and satellite technology communication are novel technological tools. As an integrated approach these two old and new technologies are now able to work together in the form of Worldwide Web or networked world—a massive infrastructure of interconnected telephone services, standardized computing hardware, the Internet, radio and television which reach every corner of the globe.

India is in transition period as far as the ICT implementation is concerned. Many good e-governance projects are coming up to facilitate people with technologically developed society. With new technology of ICT, implemented through Intranet and Web based tools, there is connectivity to bridge across isolated islands of knowledge. Knowledge presupposes human mind. The existence of individual is the basic prerequisite to apply the term knowledge. Knowledge Management as not exhaustively defined term is the subject of much literature, discussion, planning and some amount of action.

A culture of knowledge sharing needs to be introduced first and building knowledge maps can be strengthened later. For this purpose, integrated knowledge sharing programmes need to be stimulated. A cultural shift needs to be created to encourage knowledge sharing. Programmes like integrated multi-disciplinary programmes, emphasis on team problem solving that promote building a supportive culture for knowledge sharing need to be encouraged. Role of knowledge management promotes the vision of concerned sector be it agriculture, industry, business, etc., and strengthens the capacity building of the same.

As the basic principle of KM is to deal with people, culture and technology, it is generated and can also be applied in the mind of the knower. The more significant distinction in two categories of knowledge lies in distinction of tacit and explicit knowledge. Tacit knowledge is highly personal. It is very hard to formalize and, therefore, it is difficult, if not impossible to communicate.

Information and Communication Technology (ICT) has a versatile role and changed the scenario of information transactions and facilitated new forms of interactions. The broader application of ICT has paved way to the new social situations and has emphasized in shaping the public mindset and attitude towards the latest technology. Investment in ICT offers the potential for developing countries to expand exports, create good jobs and diversify their economies. The benefit of adopting ICT is that it supports a wide range of human activities and it offers a means of breaking barriers to knowledge, civic participation, and social and economic opportunity (UNDP Human Development Report, 2001).

Although ICT has the potential of assisting development efforts, its effectiveness depends on appropriate deployment. An explicit focus on using appropriate ICT for development goals may allow countries to achieve a wide diffusion of benefits and contribute to both broad-based economic growth and specific development goals. The success of national ICT strategies requires the coordination of all actors involved, from local to national to global levels (Digital Opportunity Initiative, 2001). India can use ICT in two basic ways: ICT as a production sector and ICT as a socio-economic development enabler. A number of State governments have initiated e-governance projects and many of them have been successful. Most of these are essentially for improving the service delivery and improving the government services.

Although the various States initiated their Information Technology (IT) applications 10 to 20 years ago, it is only in recent years that their governments have begun to formulate their own strategies for developing the IT sector (Government of Maharashtra 1998; Government of Tamil Nadu, 1997; Government of Andhra Pradesh, 1999). The importance of concerted strategies to cope with the rapid growth in the ICT sector and to compete with other States for more private investment has been realized. In 1997, Karnataka was the first State to present an information technology policy to attract private investment. Several others followed suit. Maharasthra and Tamil Nadu have been successful in attracting private investors to software exports and in implementing local ICT projects.

Karnataka leads India in software exports and the electronics industry, and was the first State in the country to have a software park. The Bangalore Software Park is the first to offer software services, Information Service Provider (ISP) services, training and consultancy, videoconferencing, and is the first park with International Standards Organization (ISO) certification (Naidu, 1999). Karnataka State has taken a firm step that Information Technology should be utilized to usher in an era of Electronic Governance aimed at demystifying the role of government, simplifying procedures, bring in transparency, making need based, good quality and timely information available to all citizens and providing all services in an efficient and cost-effective way and identified services on an on-time basis. The e-governance in Karnataka can help to bridge the gap between rich and the poor, between the more developed and the less developed, between the urban and the rural population by providing equal opportunities in a more meaningful way and also by empowering the less privileged sections of society.

Initially, Government of Karnataka felt that implementation of IT and to achieve effective e-governance, it may be difficult to mobilize political will, a change of mindset at various levels, administrative dedication and strategic partnership with the private sector and participation of citizens as stakeholders. The Government expected that it may be resisted by the traditionalists and those whose vested interests are threatened by the new IT policy. However, the concept of ICT was well received with the most sincere and positive manner in the State. This initial take off has influenced for further percolation down to the most underprivileged sections of society.

The goal of IT department is to "enhance and promote the use of information and communication technologies in the functioning of the government in order to make required information available to all citizens and to provide all services in an efficient way and identified services on an on-line basis". It has also addressed important issues like language, security systems, authentication etc., in order to achieve the objective of ultimate integration and a secure, user-friendly system is not lost sight off.

The Department of Information Technology, which monitors and spearheaded the entire system of ICT, operated as the nodal agency supporting every government department in their activities helping them to implement project successfully. In fact, some of the projects that span various departments are directly implemented by the IT department projects, viz., *Mukhya Vahini* (provides complete details of various programmes implemented by all the State government department for the Chief Minister's review), *Education Department* (provides documents, examines results and allows the students and their parents together to choose the college and the course in a systematic manner), *Khajane* (Treasury-tracks all the cheques on a real-time basis), *Bhoomi* (The record of Rights, Tenancy and Crops (RTC)), *Therige* (Commercial Tax-transactions at check posts), *Sachivalaya Vahini* (to track letters and files at Secretariat), *SAARIGE* (Computerization of Bangalore City Regional Transport Office), *Krishi Marata Vahini* (the first online system in India, enables 24-hour automatic collection and dissemination of market arrival and prices from the markets irrespective of geographical location), *Raitha Mitra* (Under this Raitha Mitra

Scheme, *Raitha Samparka Kendra* (Farmers Communication Centres) has been installed across the State).

KM Implementation : Success Story of Raitha Mitra Yojane

The agricultural sector in Karnataka has taken the advantage of the benefits of modern technology. With globalization of Indian agriculture and WTO agreement Indian farmers have to compete with other advanced countries. Information technology has embraced all the areas including agriculture. Raitamitra website a Cyber Extension caters to the needs of extension functionaries and farmers in general. The *http://raitamitra.kar.nic.in* is designed, developed and hosted in Kannada by National Informatics Centre for the Department of Agriculture. The website giving basic information requirement for the farmers on daily basis giving tips and information to farmers and Krishi Marata Vahini, giving online market rates on the same day, developed for Department of Agricultural Marketing.

Raita Mitra Yojane was a demand driven agricultural extension system implemented during 2000-01 in the entire State. The scheme is aided by both State and Centrally sponsored funds. At the State level, Commissioner for Agriculture is the implementing authority. The major achievement of Raitha Mitra Yojane was that it has replaced the earlier T&V system of Agricultural Extension. The agricultural extension centres opened under this programme at village level are called Raitha Samparka Kendra (RSK). The major objectives of the RSK were hereunder :

- To provide updated information on crop production options, practices and markets etc.
- To facilitate on site provision of critical inputs like seeds, bio-fertilizers, micronutrients, etc.
- To provide primary seed and soil testing facilities.
- To provide a forum for on-farm demonstration about adoption technologies developed by both public and private sector agencies.

Raitha Samparka Kendras were established at *hobli* (sub-block) level to meet the requirements of the farming communities. Presently RSK is functional in all the 745 *hoblis* existing in 176 talukas across 27 districts of the State. An Agricultural Officer duly supported by Assistant Agricultural Officers and Agricultural Assistants regularly monitors it. The strength of the supporting officer depends on the cropping intensity, irrigation facilities, and crop diversification, etc., of the *hobli*.

To harness the results of development in the field of information technology, the websiste *http://www.raitamitra.kar.nic.in* was launched by the State government on 27th February, 2001. Every RSK is provided with a telephone and a computer system with printer having an Internet Facility. The computer system is used for display of CDs on the adopted innovative practices and technologies. Internet facilities are utilized to know the latest prices at various APMC yards through Marata Vahini website *www.maratavahini.nic.in*. The website is totally user friendly with most of the informations made available in State language (Kannada). The on-line Agricultural Commodities Price Information System has turned out to be a treasure house for farmers. The arrivals, minimum, maximum and modal prices of over 100 agricultural commodities and 2000 varieties on sale at the 142 Agricultural Produce Market Committees (APMCs) are available on Internet by 4 PM everyday. Media are using this portal for further dissemination of market prices. This website is acting as an important information tool to both farmers and extension functionaries. It is regularly updated with weather forecast, market information and package of practice for various crops. The information on positioning of crucial inputs like fertilizers and seed is provided through this web.

Farmer can visit the Raitha Samparka Kendras during the working hours to get any information regarding the inputs, cultural practices, marketing avenues, commodity prices at different APMC yards, technical suggestion and know-how of the innovative farming practices. The farmer was also given an option for tele-enquiry. Databases of queries attended by RSK officials are maintained in an "Interaction register" which specifies the farmer details, purpose of his visit and the suggestion prescribed by the technical officer. Apart from attending to specific farmer queries, the technical staff also visit the villages during the pre-drawn schedule of visits and undertake field visits to provide technical guidance in adoption of proven technologies. They also communicate certain technologies through on-farm demonstration trails.

In order to make the scheme self-sustained, user charges are collected from the farmers and various public and private sector companies involved in agricultural activities. The approved user charges levied for the various services provided at RSK are listed in Table 9.1. The user charges are retained at the RSK level for promoting extension activities in the same area. As on 31st January, 2004, a sum of Rs. 2,62,25,703 (Rupees Two crores, sixty two lakhs, twenty five thousand, seven hundred and three only) is collected as service charges which is retained at the respective RSKs for their strengthening and to take up trails etc., whenever required.

Table 9.1 : Menu of Service Charges Rendered at RSK

Sl. No.	*Facilities*	*Service Charges (Rs.)*
1.	Seed sample testing	5.00 per sample
2.	Soil sample testing	3.00 per sample
3.	Rentals for the space to stock and sale agricultural inputs by the public sector and private sector companies	100.00 per month
4.	Rentals for the space used for demonstration purpose by the public sector and private sector companies (for a plot of 3m x 30m dimension)	300.00 per plot for a period of four months
5.	Rentals for promotional activities conducted in the premises of the RSK's by the public sector and private sector companies	100.00 per day per event
6.	Service charges for sale of seeds and other inputs	8 per cent of net value

It is also proposed to widen the extension services at RSKs by converging the activities of line departments like horticulture, sericulture, etc. and make single delivery point for all agriculture related activities. Reliance Petrochemicals Ltd., have come forward to establish their retail outlets in selected RSKs to supply petrol and diesel to farmers at subsidized rates. The proposal is likely to be launched in near future.

In order to document the first-hand information study team visited the Agriculture Department, Kagalipura RSK, on-farm demonstration plot of SRI cultivation adopted by a progressive farmer under the technical guidance of RSK officials and interviewed few farmers who were availing these facilities.

Additional Director of Agriculture (Human Resource Development), Department of Agriculture, Bangalore expressed that RSK has come in a big way from the farmers point of view. Through RSK we are providing daily basis relevant informations and tips on various crops and agronomic practices and preventive measures to be taken and other guidelines about seeds and fertilizers. The weather report obtained from Meteorological Department with forecasting is passed on to the farmers through RSK. During monsoon seasons to avoid spurious seeds, pesticides and fertilizers, we are providing the genuine inputs at their *hobli*, which has reduced the cost incurred in procuring the inputs and availability of genuine material to meet the satisfaction of the farmer. The most vital role of RSK is to list out the Frequently Asked Questions (FAQs) that enables farmers to get ready reckoner to clarify their doubts answered by going through this question bank.

A farmer who has utilized the services of RSK opined that instead of spending time at the petty shop discussing about the present day political scenario, if we happened to sit at RSK for few minutes, we could learn vital information regarding the farming. Earlier, they used to visit Bangalore city to get good quality seeds and pesticides during which the transportation cost and miscellaneous expenses were to be added to the actual price of the products. But now we were able to obtain similar material at no addition burden on the small and marginal farmers.

When asked for a comment on the SQI cultivation, the adopted farmer addressed that it would have been for the first time that farmers of his calibre were also noticed by the agriculture department officials. This change was noticed only after the implementing of RSK. Due to this SRI cultivation, the farmers who are deprived of irrigation could also raise the paddy cultivation with limited water resources.

Limitations of the RSK

- Low voltage and lack of continuous supply of power is the major problem. To overcome, every unit has been provided with the UPS which can work for a very limited period. Perhaps, solar connectivity can solve the problem to the possible extent.

- The information provided on MARKFED website is not real time information. The information may be a day or two old. Updating of information is very crucial.

Advantages

- As informed by the users, it provides information of input suppliers and market prices.
- It also provides information on suitable crops for the season, crop production techniques, occurrence of pest and diseases and their control measures, etc.
- Live specimens of different types of fertilizers, pests, diseases, infected crops, etc, are displayed to educate the farmers visiting the RSK.
- RSK provides the market information and also suggest the more economical market for their produce.
- RSK encourage the farmers to go for diversified cropping pattern and systems. They also suggest the new crops based on their local resources (soil type, nutrient status, rainfall pattern, climatic conditions and market availability).

Lessons Learnt

- The innovative technology should be simple, easy to access and beneficial to the end users.
- The SRI cultivation of paddy is promoted through playing the CDs in the RSK with the concept of seeing is believing, which has minimized the exposure visit cost on the department.

In the process of information communication the two ends of the transaction, the giver and the receiver exist with the core item information around which the entire process is circled. How best the information is communicated that much perfect would be received by the beneficiary. To hike the beneficiaries, the ICT tools should be user friendly and easy accessibility, affordability and ought to be made to divert the attention of the rural people approach without fear and doubt. As communication and information are interrelated changes in concepts towards development give new dimensions to theories and practices of communication. There should be keen handling of information dissemination tools that should match best to serve the purpose.

REFERENCES

Chawla, Rajeev 2003, Programmes for Roll out of Successful e-Governance Projects—*Bhoomi*—A Case Study. Department of Information Technology, Government of Karnataka, Bangalore.

Digital Opportunity Initiative. (2001), Creating a Development Dynamic, Final Report of the *Digital Opportunity Initiative.*

Liebowitz, Jay. (2001), *Knowledge Management: Learning from Knowledge Engineering, London,* CRC Press, 139.

Mithra, Raja, *Emerging State level ICT Development Strategies* The World Bank, 1818 H street, NW, Washington, D.C. 20433 USA. e-mail: rmmitra@hotmail.com

Naidu, B. Bangalore: An Information Technology Cluster. (1999). *Unpublished paper presented to Workshop* on IT Parks in Asia and the Role of the U.S. Investors in their Development, 14-15.

Parvin, Irin (July 2007), Information Communication Technologies in rural development in Bangladesh, *Journal of Rural Development,* 34(2), 61-88.

UNDP (United Nations Development Programmes), (2001), *Human Development Report 2001,* July, http://www.undp.org/hdr2001.

10 Importance of Knowledge Management in Rural Development

B. Ravi

1. Introduction

Knowledge management deals with knowledge-friendly environments in which knowledge can develop and flourish to provide individuals, organizations or regions with context-sensitive knowledge. Knowledge management is rapidly developed due to development of information and communication technology. The ICT tools help the concept of knowledge management in exchanging data, information and documents. Knowledge management is a system for managing to gather, organize, refine, analyze and disseminate knowledge in all forms within an organization, and is the ability to create and retain greater value. Knowledge can be broadly classified into explicit knowledge and tacit knowledge. Individuals are able to express through various means of communication is explicit knowledge whereas the knowledge possessed by the individual and is unable to articulate and express is called tacit knowledge. Knowledge management is not made easier by the fact that most of the valuable knowledge within organization is tacit, held within people's heads, rather than explicit, stored in files and documents.

Knowledge management is about people, relationships and a new way of working together as an entity in an organizational setting. The rural development is a process leading to sustainable improvement in the quality of life of rural people, especially the poor. The knowledge management has great potential to rural development by enhancing rural people's opportunities by improving their access to agriculture information, markets, health, and education.

2. Knowledge Management in Rural Development

The knowledge management in rural development is a dissemination of knowledge for the development of rural people through experience, values, contextual information, expert insight on rural specialization and grounded intuition that provides an environment and framework for evaluating and incorporating new experiences and information. The most fundamental aspect of knowledge management in rural development is visibility and vocabulary. Visibility gives the easy access to the rural knowledge as and when they require, and the vocabulary helps to improve the knowledge of rural people in participating the meetings, workshops, seminars, etc. The knowledge management should be addressed structurally in creating a network of rural organizations to maximize the use of both tacit and explicit knowledge.

3. Principles of Knowledge Management in Rural Development

- Building a good relationship among rural community;
- Creating a shared knowledge based by conducting training, workshops, etc.;
- Providing adequate atmosphere for sharing the ideas;
- Providing an opportunity to share the ideas among the rural people;
- To encourage the sharing of creative knowledge;
- To implement the incentives, who shares the knowledge;
- To generate the resources for rural development;
- Inculcate the reading habits among the rural community; and
- To share the internal resources, knowledge and services.

4. Knowledge Management Centre for Rural Development

Various government and non-governmental organizations are contributing the knowledge for the improvement of rural areas in establishing their respective Knowledge Management Centres.

5. Features of Knowledge Management Centres

Some of the features of the knowledge management Network are :

- The knowledge centre creates content related to Agriculture, Animal Husbandry, education, employment, health, government announcements, e-commerce and income generating enterprises, general information and environment.
- To create information about the quality management system, information related to different projects, related best practices and lessons learned, technology related white papers and tutorials.
- To develop searchable repositories.
- Global access of information.
- Content based arrangement.
- A helpdesk in different places for facilitating process consulting to problems.
- A resource on frequently asked questions by the rural community.
- Case studies and templates for proposals and newsletters are also captured in the knowledge centre.
- A role based access privilege model that ensures that every user has access only to information pertaining to his/her interest.

6. Requirement for Knowledge Management Centre

The Knowledge Management Centres could play a catalytic role in developing rural areas which require some basic needs:

(a) Technology Infrastructure

The network of knowledge centres will need to have a minimum level of connectivity and processing power and the technical skill for ongoing management and maintenance.

(b) Local Organisational Set-up

Knowledge centres have the local capacity to identify service and information need to have the skills to access and process the information and services as they are made available.

(c) Implementation of the Services and Information

There is a need to be the organised development of groups to work through and with the knowledge centres and the extension worker, to receive the information and service and to implement this in their own lives, that of their families and of their communities.

(d) Organizational Capacity

Use of localized external information to specific services is necessary to compile and develop its own information resources.

(e) Capacity to Mount and Deliver Information

The information is delivering on various modalities of the net, particularly e-mail, the WWW and chat. The service provider should be capable of keeping abreast of ongoing technology development and to undertake limited Research and Development activity in support of their work.

(f) A Human Capacity to Mobilize Resources

The communities need access to appropriate leadership and leadership training to assist in pursuing technology-enabled opportunities as they emerge.

(g) Development Capability

To integrate and expedite the various requirements, to seek out funding as required, and to ensure that the various components of the system work together smoothly.

(h) Ensure Evaluation and Feedback

To ensure evaluation and feedback from the service and information back to the information source and development group.

7. Conclusion

The knowledge management centres are creating the contents related to Agriculture, Animal Husbandry, Education, Employment, Health, Government announcements, income generating enterprises, general information and environment. A coordinated network of knowledge centres acting as Rural Development delivery nodes could be a powerful resource for supporting rural sustainability by enabling accurate information about local agricultural matters, and by facilitating cooperation and interaction between organizations, institutions and communities distributed. There are various knowledge management centres existed and joined together in the form of network for the benefit of rural development. This entire knowledge management centres voluntarily involved and established based on the same vision, interested in serving the rural people.

REFERENCES

Feather, John, The Information Society: A study of Continuity and Change, London: *facet*, 2004.

http://www.networkmagazineindia.com/200502/coverstory09. shtml

http://www.thehindubusinessline.com/bline/2005/07/12/stories/2005071200770300.ht

Rollett, Herwig, Knowledge Management: Processes and Technologies, Boston: Kluwer Academic, 2003.

Scammel, Alison (ed.), Handbook of Special Librarianship and Information Work, London: *ASLIB*, 1997.

11

Village Knowledge Management in Rural Governance Systems : Opportunities and Challenges

Harekrishna Misra

1. Introduction

ICT enabled services and processes in supporting rural development initiatives in India have progressed phenomenally. Various organisations in government, non-government and private sectors are in the process of implementing various projects relating to rural development. NeGP is geared for providing citizen centric services through 100,000 CSCs with a financial outlay of around Rs. 15,000 crores and is expected to be completed by September 2008..The Village Resource Centres (VRC) established by the Indian Space Research Organisation (ISRO), e-choupals of ITC, various e-government projects, State-wise Area Networks (SWAN) are also being implemented with the mandate to support rural development in India (Bhatnagar, 2004; Mishra and Gachhayat, 2004; Satyanarayana, 2004). The latest in the chain is Mission-2007 (Mission, 2007) which is conceptualised by MSSRF foundation. Mission-2007 is aimed to make each village a knowledge centre with the help of ICT and adding value through the CSCs, VRCs. It is said that CSCs, VRCs and VKCs would offer an ambient condition where villagers, service providers would collaborate and harness the knowledge created through these centres. CSCs, VRCs and VKCs can play a major role in optimising transaction and coordinating costs in the supply chain that are mostly due to poor connectivity, information deprivation and poor dissemination of local knowledge. National Alliance Mission recommends that SWANs should go to villages. VKCs are expected to be the facilitating centres for community based knowledge management.

It is, therefore, important that VKCs are considered as critical to rural governance and it is now imperative to understand the opportunities and challenges that exist for the agencies to implement the concept. In this chpater we discuss attributes of knowledge, its requirement and delivery systems to manage rural development issues. Organisation of the chapter is as follows. In section two various attributes of knowledge and role of ICT to manage the knowledge are discussed. It is argued that it is essential to understand distinction between information and knowledge before specifying its deliveries at the village level. In section three, we present the scenario of the ICT infrastructure in the Indian context. This is essential since Mission 2007 expects a robust ICT and related infrastructure to make a village knowledge centre functional in each village. Opportunities and challenges for providing demand-driven knowledge services through village knowledge centres are also discussed here. In section four, a framework is presented which could be used to harness knowledge in village level through a participatory approach. The objective is to support the village knowledge centre with a demand driven knowledge management service capability.

2. Data, Information, Knowledge and ICT

It is always a matter of debate to provide an expressed boundary among data, information, knowledge and their relationship with the ICT as a technology (Hahn and Subramani, 2000). Data are considered to be bare facts based on which certain analyses are done. But it is perhaps prudent to consider that facts are also relative to one's wisdom. It is also relative to the context or a situation in which the data are being collected and collated. This also requires certain amount of knowledge to bring quality to the data sets. Software engineering domains are intended to qualitatively drive the databases and their management through explicit knowledge bases. These intertwined relationships make things complex to appreciate any boundary among these three important aspects of decision making process, i.e., data, information and knowledge. While it is important to note that information is a contextual presentation of facts (data !), knowledge is an abstracted representation of the analyses carried on the information.

Generally information is a discrete version of data and knowledge gradually manifests the information with cognitive analyses of these discrete elements. Therefore, knowledge is a complex phenomenon. It depends on a number of factors which determine the nature of knowledge management involving its creation and sharing. Knowledge in information systems parlance is generally typed as tacit or explicit. Tacit knowledge has a potential to determine personal quality that makes it hard to articulate or communicate. It is also termed as the knowing or the deeply rooted know-how that emerges from action in a particular context. But explicit knowledge is termed as an expressible component that can be displayed in some predetermined form. This can be extracted from the knowledge holder and shared with other individuals (Hahn and Subramani, 2000). In many situations tacit and explicit knowledge need to collaborate for larger synergy. They need to be mutually dependent to reinforce quality of knowledge (Polyani, 1975). At times tacit knowledge forms the background to appreciate and interpret explicit knowledge. Further, knowledge is perceived to be individual as well as group driven leading to situation where organizational knowledge can be created which could toggle between tacit and explicit modes (Nonaka, 1994). Therefore, processes of knowledge creation, linkages between individuals and sharing among groups are quite dynamic and have relevance in rural development context (Brown and Duguid, 1991). In Indian context, villages and communities have their own unique and context-specific knowledge exchange mechanisms. They have various ways to network among themselves to meet their needs.

Since knowledge is personalized, it is difficult to manage individual rural household. This is because of their limited view to importance and relevance of knowledge to their livelihoods. It may, therefore, be strategically correct to provide a group-centric approach to manage their aspirations to acquire, share knowledge. This strategy looks for a support of ICT enabled environment. In Table 11.1 use of ICT in managing knowledge is presented.

As explained in Table 11.1, perspectives of knowledge provide us a gamut of inputs to appreciate its linkages to ICT. Knowledge and its management consist of dynamic and continuous set of inputs, processes which can be cognitively assimilated through an individual, group as well as an organisation. Organisations,

Table 11.1: Knowledge and ICT

Knowledge Perspectives		*Implications for Knowledge Management (KM)*	*Implications for ICT Intervention*	*Role of Information Systems*
Knowledge *vis-à-vis* data and information	Data is facts, raw numbers. Information is processed/interpreted data. Knowledge is personalized information.	KM focuses on exposing individuals to potentially useful information and facilitating assimilation of information	ICT can be extended to help in user assimilation of information	Creation of Information Infrastructure, Databases and Transaction Processing Systems, Data Warehousing
State of mind	Knowledge is the state of knowing and understanding.	KM involves enhancing individual's learning and understanding through provision of information	Role of IT is to provide access to sources of knowledge rather than knowledge itself	Expert Systems, Executive information Systems, Decision Support systems, Data Mining
Object	Knowledge is an object to be stored and manipulated.	Key KM issue is building and managing knowledge stocks	Role of IT involves gathering, storing, and transferring knowledge	
Process	Knowledge is a process of applying expertise.	KM focus is on knowledge flows and the process of creation, sharing, and distributing knowledge	Role of IT is to provide link among sources of knowledge to create wider breadth and depth of knowledge flows	
Access to information	Knowledge is a condition of access to information.	KM focus is organized access to and retrieval of content	Role of IT is to provide effective search and retrieval mechanisms for locating relevant information	
Capability	Knowledge is the potential to influence action.	KM is about building core competencies and understanding strategic know-how	Role of IT is to enhance intellectual capital by supporting development of individual and organizational competencies	Knowledge Warehouse, Knowledge Networks, Neural Networks, Fuzzy Systems

Adapted from Alavi, and Leidner, (2001).

groups and individuals are progressively harnessing the benefits of ICT in managing their inputs, processes, resource based as well as cognitive capabilities. Various systems are now conceptualised, deployed to support knowledge management exercises and some of these are "transaction process systems, expert systems, executive information systems, decision support systems" to manage various aspects of managerial as well cognitive processes. Fuzzy systems, data mining and data warehousing systems are hastening these ICT enabled processes for knowledge management. But role of ICT needs to be appreciated with the fact that its delivery is limited to mostly optimisation of cost of sharing data, information. Therefore, it is necessary to evolve sustainable information systems which can cater to the temporal needs of knowledge management imperatives of an individual, group as well as organisation as well. This calls for a systemic approach to harness knowledge among individuals, provide a networked environment so as to facilitate collaboration and sharing of information and knowledge. The said environment applies to rural community in India, essentially because of the fact that rural sector still faces poor information infrastructure to add value to the local content and adding value to this knowledge. The environment for them is very much temporal and, therefore, it is imperative that they get instant access to people and their ideas and continuous awareness and learning in a supportive community. ICT, therefore, can support knowledge management strategy through dissemination of tacit and explicit knowledge; making knowledge work invisible (integrating all the resources and stakeholders in a logical space), building relationships so that knowledge can flow. In Figure 11.1, a strategy to mediate all the knowledge sources is presented through possible ICT intervention opportunities.

Studies indicate that group activities provide a better ambience in knowledge sharing and rural communities display cohesiveness in their social and cultural activities. They are rich in their individual traditional knowledge as well as community based traditional knowledge mostly in the form tacit knowledge. This is primarily inherited. Such semantic memories need to be harnessed and captured through knowledge management systems so as to build a sustainable library of episodic memory[1] at the village level. Besides, individuals in villages have explicit knowledge in varying intensity due to social, political as well as economic activities in

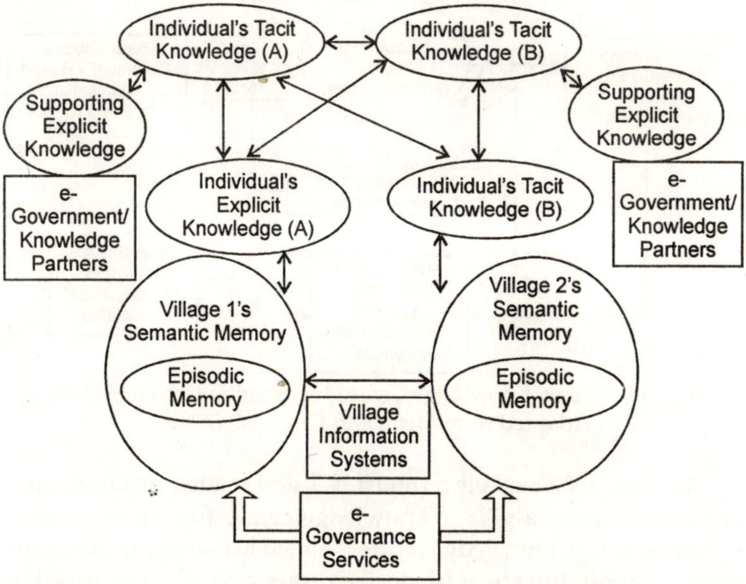

Fig. 11.1: Knowledge Transfer through Village Information Systems Adapted from Alavi, and Leidner, (2001).

the market. Rural development related interventions are increasing the levels of explicit knowledge. Various e-government services, interventions through public and private partnerships are aiding the process of transferring knowledge. This provides scope to capture them for developing local knowledge centres which can collaborate among individuals, communities and villages for sharing. This is possible through a village knowledge centre.

2.1 *Architecture of Village Knowledge Centres and ICT Infrastructure*

Various e-governance, e-government, e-business models, etc., have hastened the development process in India and have shown the way to provide support through their explicit knowledge at the village level. Most of the transactions are now being geared for execution at local level. Public-private-partnerships are now being planned through NeGP so as to create entrepreneurship environment at the village level.

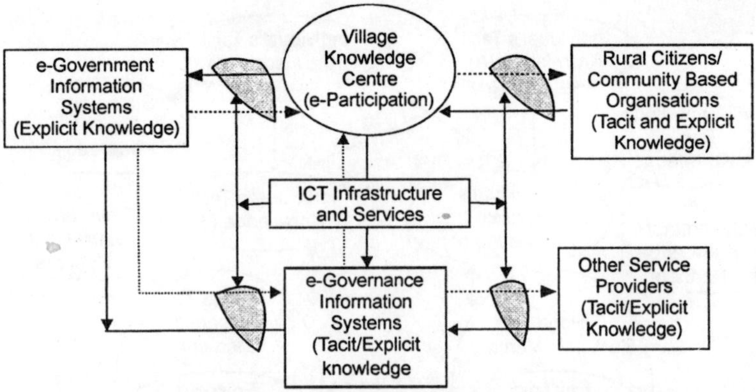

Fig. 11.2: Village Knowledge Centre-Information Driven Systems
Adapted from Misra and Hiremath (2006)

Mission 2007 expects a robust ICT and related infrastructure in order to make a village knowledge centre functional in each village. A village knowledge centre is aimed to manage the episodic memory, collaborate with individuals and groups to elicit information and store for knowledge sharing. In Figure 11.2 a framework is presented through which it is argued that Community Based Organisations (CBO), individuals should collaborate in the process of creating a Village Knowledge Centre (VKC). In the architecture of VKC, it is imperative to include villages, community based organisations in the village and individuals to collaborate and share their semantic as well episodic knowledge for greater synergy. This synergy is expected to support the rural livelihood systems in the village level.

2.1.1 Transactions and VKC

In the context of feasible and dynamic rural livelihood options, the rural citizens are subjected to transactions with various markets such as labour, land, water, financial (institutional and non-institutional), farm input and output, information, etc. These dynamic sets of transactions make the information systems for the VKC complex. Major attributes of a transaction are its "place", "time and latency" and "mode". These attributes provide an indication to understand effectiveness of the transactions. It is, therefore, essential to appreciate and record the demand of rural citizens at local level. A suitable local governance system interface is also necessary to support the individuals as well as groups like Self-Help Groups (SHG) in managing their transaction well and on time to receive desired information and services to augment their livelihood. This is possible through explicit knowledge transfer to the VKC. Role of e-government systems, public as well private agencies to collaborate in the VKC is of paramount importance.

2.1.2 Processes and VKC

Rural livelihood systems generally embrace age old and inherited traditional practices that have been accepted as per local conditions. These tacit knowledge drive practices and village level processes are mostly non-remunerative. Therefore, it is imperative that VKC develops episodic knowledge based in the village with the help of e-government systems and share it among villagers and CBOs. Collaboration among other socio-cultural communities and knowledge sharing becomes important here and role of VKC also is critical to manage and show case best practices for knowledge dissemination.

2.1.3 Information, Knowledge and VKC

Rural livelihood systems face myriad of problems associated with farm inputs, process knowledge, technology adoption, productivity, output marketing. In rural areas small and marginal farmers face socio-economic challenges due to poverty, lack of cost effective credit facilities. These summarily lead to livelihoods insecurities. One of the major attributes for such problems is "lack of information and knowledge". Knowledge on resources, support services related to livelihood goal and goal related citizen metrics is essential. Information systems help in minimizing these constraints through right sizing the information-processing environment with a proper information structure. Role of e-governance is critical here to interface with the VKC. Participatory Rural Appraisal (PRA) helps in recognizing the demand for information and, therefore, provides a support for preparation of information structure. For example, income generating option for supporting livelihood needs a complex and dynamic approach such as tracing various markets, locating demand, and reaching these sources. Here, information systems can be evaluated depending on the infrastructure available such as communication, data transfer, data access, power, applications such as information portal and maintaining these sources on a sustainable basis.

3. ICT Enabled VKC: Challenges and Opportunities

Feasibility of VKCs needs to be assessed on the basis of ICT infrastructure policies. ICT infrastructure needs active support of IS infrastructure. Success of VKC mostly lies with purposeful governance systems that drives the IS infrastructure in India. In Table 11.2 status of ICT and IS infrastructure is presented.

Table 11.2: Indices for the ICT Infrastructure in India

Sl. No.	Name of Index	Rank of India (Nations Surveyed)				
		2004-05 (104)	2005-06 (115)	2006-07 (122)	2007-08 (127)	2008-09 (134)
1.	Network Readiness Index	39	40	44	50	54
	Individual readiness	44	50	37	46	45
	Business readiness	36	29	52	28	27
	Government readiness	34	28	28	45	57
2.	Usage Component Index	42	46	39	51	59
	Individual Usage	85	114	107	109	114
	Business Usage	23	27	20	26	30
	Government	23	32	36	40	47
3	Environment Component Index	38	40	46	54	60
	Market environment	27	37	28	49	50
	Political and regulatory	33	30	48	47	57
	Infrastructure	86	96	63	71	76
4.	ICT Spending	64	41	27	56	88

Source: Global IT Report.

ICT readiness in India is fast progressing. As per global IT readiness report, however, India still much behind many countries.

At national level, there are still some areas which need attention of policy makers to promote ICT. More specifically, as presented in Table 11.2., India needs to address issues related to infrastructure, spread of ICT, availability of electricity. Individual usage of ICT also is dismally low in India. Internet bandwidth availability also is low at individual level. However, Indian Government's priority on ICT adoption is commendable. This will tremendously influence the ICT adoption scenario and there is a scope to improve upon.

However, e-government readiness that influences the IS infrastructure for VKCs is yet to build up. In Figure 11.3 status of e-government in India in global scenario is presented.

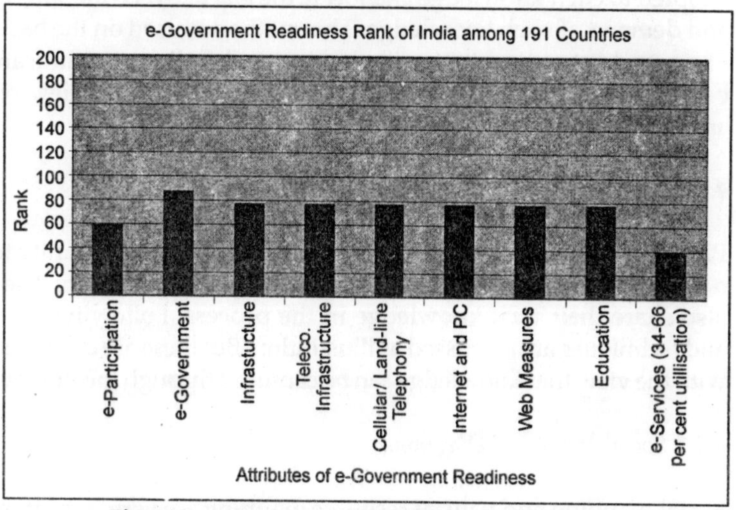

Fig. 11.3: e-Government Readiness Index in India

This poor infrastructure readiness has reflected proportionately internet penetration, PC penetration and web measures.

Despite these challenges, VKCs seem to have enough potential create opportunities. These opportunities are visible in the form of various amendments in the policy level which mandates Panchayati Raj Institutions (PRI) to participate in the decision making process at local level. Besides, VKCs are promoting an interface among various partners through public-private partnership models and NeGP extends the same philosophy.

4. An Approach to Create Village Knowledge

In this chapter VKCs are identified to be a centre to garner and provide knowledge to the local community on demand. All the agencies involved in the process are expected to collaborate to provide, disseminate knowledge so as to support the village livelihood systems. It is also viewed that garnering tacit and explicit knowledge of the local community is an important exercise for the purpose. This is imperative with the viewpoint that local community needs to collaborate, share their knowledge among themselves at the peer level. In order to create such knowledge at the village level, Participatory Rural Appraisal (PRA) method is adopted to elicit knowledge and locate the gap between the supply and demand of such knowledge. This method is used on the basis of an understanding that villagers in rural India communicate better in a mediated environment and provide holistic view on any local issue in their own language.

4.1 PRA Method

PRA method uses various tools to bring the village community to a common platform before electing data and information. They also share their tacit knowledge in the process. Following tools and techniques are discussed as illustration. But these are discussed with the view that knowledge can be captured through the process.

4.1.1 Social Maps and Diagrams

Social mapping and natural resource mapping are very important in the PRA exercise since it involves local community to assess the natural resources such as caste system, water resources, education, and religious centres. It also provides episodic knowledge on soil conditions, cropping pattern, rainfall, production and consumption pattern in the households, etc. Diagrams are drawn by participants to explain better issues of common interest. They include various kinds of maps for giving a bird's eye view of the community or zone; transects which give a horizontal view of an area or zone and act as complementary information to maps; calendars which give information on time and those changes that take place during the course of seasons and times (there are seasonal calendars, labour calendars, crop calendars and the like); historical profiles that show what important events have taken place in the life of the community; Venn diagrams that help to explore institutional information, the societal power fabric including in-village groups and organisations as well as those operating in the community from outside and their linkages. Thus, in the process semantic knowledge as well as episodic knowledge are captured.

4.1.2 Ranking and Quantification Methods

The importance of ranking and quantification tools lies in the fact that there is no need to have absolute figures for information such as people's income. In fact, informants are unlikely to share such information. For many purposes, relative rankings are just as useful and a lot less sensitive to obtain. There are times when quantification techniques are useful even when participatory appraisals are better at getting qualitative information. Here, it is the use of countable objects such as pebbles, beans and nuts to help determine quantities and magnitudes of issues.

4.1.3 Preference/Problem Ranking

Ranking gets the community to prioritise their preferences/ problems, concerns or strengths of their opinions on various issues. The first step here is to decide on what is to be ranked and/or prioritised. For example, in ranking problems it is recommended to list all problems voiced by the community. The problems are ranked taking two at a time and scores are assigned according to their priority. Probing is done to ensure that views and opinions are expressed after each comparison of pairs. After the process the scores are added and rated in order of priority resulting from individual scores by problem rated.

4.2 PRA Tools and Techniques for Knowledge Elicitation

PRA tools as discussed above are used for involving rural citizens to share information on common as well individual resources, their problems, expectations, and limitations in earning their livelihoods which is the most important issue before them. Rural citizens depend mostly on the resources available in the village; support received from the agencies like government, NGOs and Community Based Organisations (CBOs). In most cases these supports are not commensurate with their expectations and, therefore, leading to deprivation in earning the sustainable livelihood. These expectations are captured through the PRA process which attempts to deliver certain meta-measurable indicators the citizens consider to be important. In Table 11.3, application of PRA tools and expected deliveries are discussed and these expectations are mapped to define local knowledge.

PRA exercise is based on assumption that local communities are essential collaborators in the planning process. However, elicitation of their knowledge in their explainable terms is a difficult task and PRA is intended to capture the required knowledge.

In Table 11.3 six processes are discussed in order to complete the PRA exercise. Each process is intended to capture certain form of knowledge as explained by the community and individuals participating in the process. During the whole process data, information and knowledge are captured, collated and analysed which provide more authentic insights to the decision makers. Normal ICT intervened and designed process such as GIS enabled information systems, e-government applications do not provide the intended portfolio as well as demand centric knowledge delivery systems at the local level because of the implicit IS design and requirement gap. In Table 11.3, we provide the knowledge capturing methods which can be incorporated in the village information system design process.

5. Conclusion

ICT is a service enabler tool and its role in development process is well appreciated. Mission 2007 demands a knowledge management system in the village level with active interfaces among all the stakeholders and expects integration of services available through NeGP, VRCs and many more enterprise level applications. It is viewed that village knowledge centres would hasten the process of poverty alleviation with proper dissemination local knowledge coupled with need based explicit knowledge. But ICT infrastructure needs to be put in place to manage this

Table 11.3: Citizens' Metrics Elicitation through PRA Tools

PRA Process	*Knowledge Measurement*	*Knowledge Management Issues*	*Scope for ICT Intervention*	*Remarks*
Natural Resource and Social Maps	Describes present scenario of the community development plan and its impact	Semantic Knowledge	Village database, Village information system (Base line Data: Explicit and Tacit Knowledge)	GIS enabled systems can take help of these knowledge with suitable interface
Problem Tree (Cause-effect analyses)	Organising livelihood security and Development Options and Prioritisation	Semantic Knowledge	Household information system (Tacit and explicit Knowledge)	Interface with e-government (CSC), VRC and other agencies
Historical Trend (Time-Series)	Provides the trend of natural resource availability and use	Episodic Knowledge through semantic aggregation	Village information system	GIS enabled systems can take help of these knowledge with suitable interface
Venn Diagram (Mapping of relevance of)	Describes prioritisation of the social problems and social stress, perception of individuals on institutional influences (police, doctors, politicians, government systems) on their livelihood systems	Semantic Knowledge	Village information system	Interface with e-government (CSC), VRC and other agencies
Village Transect	Data validation	Information resource	Village information system	—
Village Micro-Plan	Data Creation	Semantic, and Episodic Knowledge	Village information system	Interface with e-government (CSC), VRC and other agencies

Source: Adapted from Misra *et al.*, 2006.

expectation. It is, therefore, necessary that rural communities in the village collaborate, create their own knowledge and demand necessary information from the serving agencies. Creating an atmosphere for eliciting the requirements and prioritising the needs of citizens is a complex phenomenon because of the spatial, political, social, religious and cultural dynamics. This is a challenge before the VKC to build a suitable and sustainable mechanism to encourage availability of the supply driven services with active citizens' participation. In this chapter knowledge creation is discussed as an illustration and there is a plan to conduct detailed study through action research.

NOTES

1. Long-term memory is categorised as episodic memory, which is the ability to remember specific incidents and can retrieve on demand. Semantic memory consists of meaningful facts, situations in general and forms a repository for use.

REFERENCES

Alavi, Maryam, and Leidner, Dorothy E., (2001), "Review: Knowledge Management and Knowledge Management Systems: Conceptual Foundations and Research Issues, *MIS Quarterly*, Vol. 25, No. 1, pp. 107-136, March.

Bhatnagar, Subhash, (2004), *e-government: From Vision to Implementation, A Practical Guide with Case Studies*, Sage Publications, New Delhi, pp. 60-64.

Brown, J.S., and Duguid, P. (1991), "Organizational Learning and Communities of Practice: Toward a Unified View of Working, Learning, and Innovation", *Organization Science* (2:1).

Hahn, J.; Subramani, M. (2000), "A framework of knowledge management systems: Issues and challenges for theory and practice", International Conference on Information Systems, Brisbane, Australia, pp. 302-12.

Mishra, Satyan; Nitin Gachhayat (2004) "Rural Business through ICT: Profitability and Role of Governance", paper presented in IRMA Silver Jubilee Symposium, December 14-19, Anand: Institute of Rural Management (IRMA).

Misra, H.K. and Hiremath, B.N. (2006), ICT Initiatives for Sustainable Livelihood Security: A Demand-driven Rural e-Governance

Framework For Scale-up, Working Paper 198, IRMA.

Misra, H.K.; Hiremath, B.N. and Mishra, D.P., (2006), Citizen Centric ICT Initiatives for Rural Development in Indian Context: A Participatory Framework, Working Paper 193, IRMA.

Mission 2007, Every Village A Knowledge Centre, National Convention, IGNOU Campus, New Delhi, August 1-3.

Nonaka, I. (1994), "A Dynamic Theory of Organizational Knowledge Creation", *Organization Science* (5:1).

Polanyi, M. (1975), *Personal Knowledge,* in Meaning, M. Polanyi and H. Prosch (eds.), University of Chicago Press, Chicago.

Satyanarayana, J. (2004), *e-Government, the Science of the Possible*. New Delhi: Prentice Hall of India, pp. 8-22.

12

Agro Climatic Planning and Information Bank (APIB) : A KM Initiative in Agriculture Sector

V. Madhava Rao, R.R. Hermon and *P. Kesava Rao*

Introduction

India, with a geographical area of 329 mha is bestowed with the bounties of natural resources, namely minerals, soils, water, flora and fauna, and marine resources. Over exploitation of available natural resources for meeting the increasing demand for food, fuel and fibre of ever-growing population has led to degradation of land by way of soil erosion by water and wind, salinization and alkalinisation, water logging, shifting cultivation, etc. An estimated 175 mha of land are subject to some kind of degradation. Soil erosion by water and wind alone accounts for an estimated 150 mha. In addition, water logging, soil salinization and alkalinisation, and shifting cultivation have affected an estimated 6 mha, 7.16 mha and 4.36 mha of land, respectively. Degradation of land by deforestation, forest fire, frequent floods and drought, further compounds the problem. For optimal utilization of available natural resources and for taking up any preventive or curative measures, timely and reliable information on natural resources with respect to their nature, extent and spatial distribution; and nature, magnitude and temporal behaviour of various types of degraded lands, is a prerequisite. Hitherto, such information has been generated through conventional approach using topographical sheets or aerial photographs. Synoptic view of a fairly large area provided by multi-spectral measurements made from satellite platforms at regular intervals enable generating information on natural resources, degraded lands and environment in a timely and cost-effective manner.

Agriculture constitutes the backbone of the Indian economy. With rapidly rising population, already a billion plus, threatening to make India the most populated country in the world in next few decades, one has to look towards advanced technologies to help in meeting the needs of this burgeoning population for food, fibre and fuel. There is also need for utilization of our natural resources in a sustainable manner. Remote sensing and Geomatics technologies have demonstrated the potential for assisting in the management of these precious resources. At the international level, ever since the launch of Landsat I, the first civilian remote sensing satellite in July 1972, the indispensable role of satellite remote sensing in agriculture sector has been fully appreciated. In fact, the choice of spectral bands in most of the civilian remote sensing satellites launched by various countries, including India, to-date has been dictated by their use for efficacious management of resources related to agriculture. This capability has been further enhanced manifold by Geomatics during the last few years, especially with the availability of high resolution satellite images from IRS and IKONOS satellites.

Geomatics deals with the tools/techniques related to the measurement of geographical data, the data that has both spatial and non-spatial components. Most common among these tools are remote sensing, geographical information system (GIS) and Global Positioning System (GPS). While remote sensing data provides a synoptic, multi-spectral and repetitive information about any resource, the GIS helps in integrating the various spatial thematic layers (including remote sensing data) to arrive at an integrated decision. GPS enables the user to know the precise location of a target, which may be useful in identification, mapping or precise operation. Agriculture is a resource, which has got a large geographical extent. Especially in a country like India, where agriculture is the backbone of the country, there is great need of getting spatial information about this sector. The green revolution of 1960s has made the country's food production progress remarkable. The requirement has grown from less than 50 million tonnes in 1950s to more than 200 million tonnes at present.

However, green revolution is also associated with many negative implications including the environmental degradation. Hence, in the twenty-first century, to steer the agricultural achievements towards the path of an "evergreen revolution", there is a need to blend the traditional knowledge with frontier technologies. Information and communication technology; space technology; geographical information systems (GIS) are the tools of such frontier technologies which would help in creating agricultural management systems; making plans for sustainable agriculture; and bringing new areas (through development of wastelands) into productive agriculture. This present article tries to explore the role of Geoinformatics with special emphasis on remote sensing and GIS in agricultural development.

The role of remote sensing and GIS in agricultural applications can be broadly categorized into two groups—inventorying/ mapping and management. While remote sensing data alone is mostly used for, inventorying (crop acreage estimation, crop condition assessment, crop yield forecasting, soil mapping, etc.) purposes, the management (irrigation management, cropping system analysis, precision farming, etc.) needs various other types of spatio physical environmental information. The latter has to be integrated with remote sensing data, where the functionality of GIS is used effectively for governance and for decision support.

Agro Climatic Planning and Information Bank (APIB)

Agriculture is still the primary sector in Indian economy. While, Green Revolution's food production of about 5.1 million tonnes in 1950 to over 205 million tonnes now, the higher economic growth and population pressure demands about 260 million tonnes of foodgrains by 2030. It is, therefore, imperative that an accelerated pace of food production could be possible with modern biotechnology, information technology, space technology and judicious use of natural resources.

Further critical aspects of agriculture like seeds, financial support, fetilizer, marketing support, agro-processing and post harvest technologies, etc., are expected to improve the productivity of Indian agriculture.

Agriculture reform is the need of the hour to bring better productivity through utilisation of new technology. APIB initiated in 1998, initially by ISRO, at 1: 50,000, on a pilot basis in Karnataka and subsequently in Meghalaya, for one district each, was seen as a promise by planners, nurtured by technologists and implemented by farmers. APIB with its concept of "single window" access to knowledge base in the field of agriculture sector is eminently suitable to facilitate the reform process.

One of the important facilitating factors is to enable more effective and participatory planning and decision making will be to create an access to what may be called knowledge base which has bearing on decision making and activities of various stakeholders/ users.

The final decision in agriculture rests with the cultivator. Given the local agro-climatic and land-endowments, the farmer's decisions are largely influenced by factors like availability of water, inputs, credit and overall infrastructure situation including the access to the market. Yet he has a variety of options and he exercises his choice to the best of his knowledge and ability. Hence, the farmer is in need of being aided as to what are his best options by access to a comprehensive agro plans and assessment of potential which represent these options.

This activity will not be limited to handling over the plan printed on paper but also providing with back-up information and expert advice and should be constantly updated in the light of changes in the environment and technology to fulfil the requirements sustainable agricultural land use planning.

APIB requirement is multipronged approach to develop databases to contain information on both Spatial and Non-Spatial parameters. The linkages between non-spatial and spatial databases will be facilitated through Geographical Information System (GIS). Decision Support System (DSS) provide a framework for integrating databases management systems, analytical models and graphics in order to improve decision making process.

For Crop Planning based on watershed as a unit GIS is an ideal tool since Digital Elevation Model (DEM) created in GIS can be integrated with other spatial information including land use pattern obtained from Remote Sensing Data from time to time is very important for optimizing the use of limited water resources for maximizing and sustaining the productivity under rainfed conditions.

This vision is reflected in Precision Farming aims to direct the application of Seed, Fertilizers, Pesticides and Water within fields in ways that optimize farm returns and minimize bio-pesticides and environmental hazards. Adoption of this technology requires accurate natural resources maps showing physical and chemical properties which are the tools to apply the inputs as per the spatial variability.

Thus APIB is emerging as a Knowledge Management in Agriculture Practice, making economically viable, productivity and growth oriented and integrating with the enrichment in the progress and livelihood of common men.

Project Objectives

The APIB Project primarily aims at addressing the following objectives :

1. To prepare agriculture and natural resources inventories by analysis of temporal satellite data, including agricultural land use/land cover; cropping systems; irrigated crop land; soils; degraded land; geomorphology; ground water potential; drainage characteristics; cultural features; etc.
2. To collect agro-climatic and agricultural data for agro-ecological characterisation and agri-climatic regional planning.
3. To develop a database for Agricultural Practices, Seeds, Fertilizers, Plant Protection, Agricultural Implements, Agricultural Credits, Insurance Schemes, Subsidy, Agriculture Market Infrastructure, Weather Information, Socio-economic infrastructure, in GIS.
4. Development of Spatial Decision Support System (SDSS) for agro-climatic planning and information bank for agricultural reform process as well as the management of agricultural land and other agricultural allied activities.
5. Suggesting sustainable agricultural land use plan based on integration of land capability, land productivity, soil suitability, terrain characteristics and socio-economic, etc., information using GIS.

Study Area

The study area is currently for Champawat and Dehradun District of the Uttarakhand State and to be subsequently extended to other districts. The information bank extends up to village level with soil profiling and mapping up to micro level applications, useful for decision making in agriculture sector, linking all related sectors of rural economy.

Methodology

APIB is expected to play an important role in the agricultural reform process and in developing agricultural planning and development. It established linkages with various organisations, efforts made in synthesizing of data, dissemination of planning advice and information modules developed for serving the diverse user clientele in the agriculture sector.

Agro-Climatic and Natural Resources Database

In order to achieve the various objectives envisaged under APIB, an assessment of its clientele's planning needs in the field of agriculture, viz., farmers, rural financial institutions, input / output traders, agricultural researchers, extension workers, planners, etc., are required to be studied and analysed. Based on the needs expressed by the user clientele, APIB has followed a multipronged approach to develop databases. As a first step, APIB has designed a database structure to contain information on both spatial and non-spatial elements. For example, in the non-spatial domain, APIB information system contains modules on fertilizers, plan protection, seeds/seedlings, package of practices, agricultural implements, climatological data, credit/insurance schemes available, infrastructure for processing and marketing, demographic details, etc. Similarly, in the spatial domain, it has information on various resources like land use, groundwater, soils, slope, etc.

(a) Non-Spatial Data Base : Given below is a brief summary of APIB non-spatial database, which shall be generated for the four districts of Uttaranchal State :

(i) *Package of Practices Module* : Package of practices collected for all major crops like cereals, pulses, cash crops, oil seeds, fodder crops, fruit crops, spices, vegetables, floriculture, medicinal and aromatic plants, etc. Package of practices are also available for many high-yield hybrids produced by many private companies. Value addition in the form of recent market prices, support prices, inputs suppliers, etc., are being developed.

(ii) *Seeds/Seedlings Module* : This will contain information on the special characteristics/salient features including information like yield, resistance to pests/diseases, quantity of seeds required, crop duration, crop suitability for different regions, packing and price information and dealer network in the priority districts.

(iii) Fertilizers Module : The module will have detailed information on type of fertilizers, and their technical formula, commercial trade names, prices and dealers network in the priority districts. The software package for recommending fertilizer dosage based on soil test and crop type shall be developed.

(iv) *Plant Protection Module* : Information content in this module will include the type of chemicals, their active ingredients, trade names, prices, applicability to different crops/pests, dealers/supliers, etc. This module will also contain information regarding biological pest control as well as other conventional pest control agents. In addition to the information on integrated pest management practices for selected crops and the plant projection guide for horticultural crops.

(v) *Agricultural Implements* : Under this module, APIB has information on various hand tools, bullock/tractor drawn implements, irrigation equipment, plant protection equipment, harvest and post-harvest equipment, their suppliers, price information, models, salient features, etc.

(vi) *Agricultural Credit*: Information readily available with the Banks will cover different credit schemes in agriculture and allied sectors, floated by different commercial rural banks in the districts. The details of each scheme covering information on interest rates, repayment terms, documents to be produced and other terms and conditions of schemes, location addresses of the branches of the different banks, specimen copies of applications (available for a few banks), etc., will also be available.

(vii) *Insurance for Agriculture and Allied Sectors* : This module has details of various insurance schemes for crops, plantation, agricultural implements and farm machinery, animal husbandry, including information on terms and conditions of the schemes, premium rates, eligibility criteria/procedure and benefits as well as the branch network of the insurance companies.

(viii) *Subsidy Programmes for Agriculture* : The database under this module contain vast information on the various subsidy programmes available for farming sector beneficiaries in the four priority districts of Uttaranchal. Information on actual availability procedure with details of eligibility criteria, subsidy credit components, documentation, etc., is available.

(ix) *Agriculture Market Infrastructure* : APIB has synthesized information on market infrastructure facilities in its four priority districts of Uttaranchal. This data module provides information on the network of Agriculture Produce Marketing Committees (APMC) in these districts, market charges, godown and storage facilities available and their charges. APIB will have information on export policies applicable for selected farm products. The price information for selected commodities shall also he available from Uttaranchal State Agricultural Marketing Board with whom APIB will establish a formal institutional contact for market related data exchange.

(x) *Agricultural Weather Information System* : Weather is a very critical parameter for agriculture and allied sectors. Most of the farming activities are guided by weather conditions in an area. APIB shall develop a weather information system. Based on weekly and monthly rainfall data/ moving averages for rainfall and weekly probabilities of rainfall, long term climate change and trends in rainfall patterns shall be identified for these districts.

(xi) *Training and Development* : The module has the details on types of training, periods of training, benefits as well as the locations of farmers' training centres.

(xii) *Socio-Economic Infrastructure* : The village-wise census details on demography and amenities has been collected. In addition, also block-wise infrastructural details were collected. Computerisation of basic data addresses most of the information needs, accomplished. Additonally all the relevant socio-economic information for at least the past five years are also made available.

(b) ***Spatial Database:*** The strength of APIB is a powerful state-of-the art image analysis and GIS facilities to assess the natural resources endowments of any agro-climatic region in Uttaranchal, in spatial and temporal domain, for taking decision by farmers at plot level.

Conclusion

India is at the forefront of Geoinformatics technology, while agriculture in India, is under serious stress. Modern technologies like GIS, Remote Sensing, GPS and other emerging technologies like Sensor based technologies, complementing agriculture technologies namely biotechnology, precision agriculture and modern irrigation technologies, is expected to meet the growing demand of India in food security, by improving productivity in agriculture practice and optimum use of resources, which is emerging, as a knowledge management in agriculture sector.

13
Conclusion

Practicing knowledge by the method of sharing in the process of development is the central focus which runs through all the chapters. A few authors stressed on how to build Knowledge Management (KM) as a more effective tool in developing rural areas. The crucial role by KM in Rural Governance Systems is described in detail. Some others made keen observations in developing strategies of knowledge management in dairy cooperatives. Knowledge management plays critical role in research and development of Indian agriculture. This is more elaborated with illustrations in a few articles. The role of different methods of disseminating knowledge in the process of managing information in libraries is described in detail.

Needs to develop Knowledge Repositories wherein people voluntarily come forward to elicit information and store for Knowledge Sharing in future. This not only shows the possible problems they face on their journey but also cautious against probable milestones they would face in their work process. There is an urge to develop episodic knowledge base along the line of e-government systems and share among villagers and CBOs. This could be developed by VKCs. Participatory Rural Appraisal (PRA) method has many tools which brings the village community to a common platform. This can be used to share their tacit (individual) knowledge within their community. ICT tools are helpful in making the tacit into more explicit.

Extensive utility of ICT as a service enabler tool can be practiced in developing a Knowledge Management System in the village level. ICT infrastructure needs to develop to manage for dissemination of local knowledge coupled with the need based explicit knowledge. Creating an atmosphere which collaborates rural communities in creating indigenous knowledge, requesting for information, implementing the suggestions given is need of the hour. This is the challenge for knowledge managers in rural areas to build a suitable and sustainable mechanism to encourage availability of the services with the increase in local citizen's participation. This can be planned eventually, implemented methodically and monitored critically in the form of a survey study and action research.

Index